The Ultimate

Air Fryer

Cookbook

The Best Selection of Recipes with Colored Pictures. Tips & Tricks to Fry, Grill, Roast, and Bake for Everyday Meals

Sophie Warn

Table of Contents

Introduction

Air fryers have started to become popular, due to the fact that you can avoid many of the unhealthy aspects of modern cooking. But what is an air fryer exactly, and how on earth does it work?

Air fryers are basically an upgraded, enhanced countertop oven, but they became popular for one particular reason. In fact, many of the manufacturers, such as Philips, market this machine solely based on the claim that the air fryers accurately mimic deep-frying, which, although extremely unhealthy, is still very popular in this day and age (as it is, in my opinion, one of the most delicious ways to eat food).

Air fryers work with the use of a fan and a heating mechanism. You place the food you want cooked in a basket or on the rack, turn on the machine, and the air fryer distributes oven-temperature hot air around your food. It provides consistent, pervasive heat evenly to all the food within. This heat circulation achieves the crispy taste and texture that is so tantalizing in deep fried foods, but without the unhealthy and dangerous oil! Both have been replaced by this miracle machine with hot air and a fan.

Advantages to Using an Air Fryer

I may have already slipped in a few of the advantages to using an air fryer, but now let's expand a little more on everything an air fryer can do for you. After all, no investment should be made unless it's absolutely worthwhile.

And in truth, the air fryer is very worthwhile. I cannot begin to tell you how the advantages start piling up; this is not just another average appliance that everyone is getting because of a simple trend. People are getting air fryers because of their incredible, numerous, multifaceted benefits.

There are, however, a few notable advantages of using an air fryer, which I'll list below. If you don't know anything else about air fryers, I hope that these will convince you of their worth.

Healthier Cooking

This is perhaps the top benefit that comes with air frying. In a society that really struggles with healthy cooking, we can use all the help we can get. Luckily, air fryers make it easy, all while maintaining many of the factors that make unhealthy food delicious!
Air fryers use very little oil, which is one of the best ways to replace those unhealthy fried foods, like fried chicken, potatoes, and so many others. If you are like me (a lover of deep fried foods) then this is the answer to your dilemma of healthy eating while still enjoying the crispy taste of food!

Do keep in mind that you still need to spray fried foods, such as fish, with a touch of oil to make sure it does get evenly crispy. All in all, however, there is no denying the amount of oils is a whole lot less.

This singular change makes all the difference in the world. Healthy eating has never been easier, as you'll get the same crispy and flavorsome results, with minimal amounts of added oils. You'll even be able to "fry" foods you never were able to before—the possibilities are endless!

Safer and Easier

Nothing scares me more than a hot pot of oil. It is an accident waiting to happen, and getting struck with burning oil splatters is no joke! But this, and its corresponding injuries, is often the price to pay for deep fried foods.

Air fryers are also user-friendly, and this makes a huge difference. You don't have to feel like you are studying for a degree when working with an air fryer. Making dinner is far less complicated in an air fryer than many of the traditional methods of cooking. For some meals—unless you choose one of the more complex recipes I'll share later—you can even revert to placing a small piece of meat (even if it happens to be frozen!) into the basket and select the cooking settings.

The simplicity of the air fryer is its beauty. You will save countless time and unnecessary frustrations, and still make delicious food!

Faster Than Cooking in the Oven

Once you buy an air fryer and set it to heat for the first time, you won't know what hit you! The average normal oven needs about 10 minutes to preheat. Due to the air fryer's smaller size and innovative design, it will be ready to go in no time!

It's even faster during the actual cooking. With the circulation that allows your food to be cooked crisp and even, it cuts a whole lot of cooking time out of the equation. This is amazing, especially in this day and age where technology, work, friends, family, and even pets are constantly demanding our attention.

Just imagine! You could set your food in the air fryer, and (with some recipes) it will be ready to eat in less than 20 minutes!

Saves Space

If you are someone living in a small apartment, or a student accommodation, then an air fryer is perfect for you. Air fryers are much smaller in comparison to a conventional oven and you can easily make use of this air fryer in 1 cubic foot of your kitchen.

You can even pack your air fryer away after use if need be, but the majority of people choose to keep it out on the counter. But it's nice to have the option to move your air fryer around if space becomes an issue.

Low Operating Costs

Considering how much cooking oil costs these days and the amount you need to use, you will soon be cutting costs in making deep fried foods. All an air fryer uses is a small amount of oil and some of the electricity to power up the air fryer, about the same amount that a countertop oven would.

Not only will you be cutting out the massive oil costs, which will save money, you will likely also save money by ordering out less, as you'll be able to replicate your favorite foods quickly and easily at home!

No Oil Smell

In reality, smelling like the food you just ate is not impressive, regardless of how delicious the food may be. This is what often happens, however, when people enjoy deep fried foods.

When deep frying foods, it also causes the whole house to smell, and as the oil splatters around, it can leave a massive mess. The oil can even harden on the walls, causing grime to build up into a nasty concentration of dirt and grease.

With less cooking oil, air fryers don't have any of those oil smells and keeps the space cleaner around you, as all the oils, smells, and actual cooking are contained within the machine.

Preserves Nutrients

When you are cooking your food in an air fryer, it actually protects a lot of the food from losing all its moisture. This means that with the use of a little oil, as well as circulation with hot air, it can allow your food to keep most of its nutrients which is excellent for you!

If you want to cook healthy foods with the purpose of maintaining as many nutrients as possible, then an air fryer is perfect for you!

Easier to Clean

Cleaning is perhaps the bane of my existence, especially after cooking and having a long day. This can really take away a lot of the pleasure of making yourself a great meal. But an air fryer lightens the burden by being easy to clean!

Consistent cleaning after using it (much like any pot or pan) can allow for easier and simpler living. You just need some soapy water and a non-scratch sponge to clean both the exterior and the interior of your air fryer. Some air fryers are even dishwasher-safe!

Great Flavour

The flavor of air fryer "fried" foods is nearly identical to traditional frying, and the texture is exact. You can cook a lot of those great frozen foods, such as onion rings or french fries, and still achieve that crunchy effect. This certainly can help you turn to healthier foods, especially if your goal is for healthy but quality meals.

The air fryer helps to cook your food to perfect crispness, instead of the soggy mess that happens when you try alternative methods of cooking foods that are meant to be deep fried (like chicken tenders). No one really enjoys mushy food. The air fryer keeps that desired element while remaining healthy.

All you will really need is just some cooking oil sprayed outside of your food to end up with a cooked interior and a crunchy exterior. So no worries! You still can eat your foods with a crunch and a healthier result!

Versatile

Unlike rice cookers meant just for rice, or bread makers meant just for bread, you will find that an air fryer leaves a lot of room to be both versatile and healthier. You can cook almost anything you would like in the air fryer (as long as it fits). From spaghetti squash, to desserts, even to fried chicken!
You will probably never run out of air frying options!

Various Types of Air Fryers and How to Choose the One for You

There isn't one standardized choice of air fryers, which means you are far more likely to find an air fryer that really suits your particular needs. Whether it be size or price, you have a wider variety of choices than what normally comes with conventional ovens.
So what are the key aspects that you need to take into consideration when getting yourself a nice air fryer? Let's begin:

- **Dimensions:** Obviously they come in different sizes, and despite saving space, some can still be bulky. When thinking about your countertop, you do want to consider its size and dimensions. You don't want to play a game of tilt with your air fryer, nor have it taken up all the extra space you have!

- **Safety Features:** You may want to check that it has an auto shutoff, as it is certainly a desirable feature. Air fryers can get very hot during use, and an auto-shutoff can save you a lot of stress and fire emergencies. Furthermore, having a cool exterior can prevent potential red and burnt hands. So do yourself a favor and make sure they have all these elements at hand.

- **Reviews:** Naturally, this is the best thing to check out. Considering that the businesses rarely give out all the information, you will certainly find it out when people leave reviews. The customer hides nothing, and if they are unhappy, they make sure everyone else knows about it. However, if people are very happy, many of them will also note it in the reviews, and it is best to target the air fryers that tend to have the high reviews.

Two Common Differences

Beyond those functional differences, there are two mainstream designs of air fryers: basket air fryers and oven air fryers. Each has very unique and distinguished features in which to enjoy. Let us take a look at the differences between the two:

Basket Air Fryers

Basket fryers are known to need less space than oven air fryers, which is very practical if you have limited space. Not only does it save space, but it also saves time, as the food is quickly heated up (without unnecessarily heating up the kitchen). Unlike an oven air fryer, and the larger traditional oven, it only takes about 1-2 minutes for the basket air fryer to heat up, and it is quite easy to place the foods inside of the basket.

The cons are, for one, that it does make a lot more noise than the oven air fryer. You also will not be able to watch the food as it cooks, which can increase the chances of burnt food if you are not careful. Also, a basket air fryer may not be the best if you need to cook a lot of food, as it is limited in capacity. This means that batch cooking may be required if you need a large amount of food.

This makes a basket air fryer ideal if you have a limited budget, don't need to cook a huge amount of food, and have limited free time.

They are quick, small, and convenient, especially perfect for people who are students or single working professionals, and maybe even you!

Oven Air Fryers

Oven air fryers, in contrast, have a larger capacity, which means you can cook a lot more food at the same time. They also have multiple functions for cooking and cut down on the noise than the basket air fryer. You will also be able to move the food closer or even further away from the heating element. There is a lot more flexibility involved in the use of an oven air fryer. Best of all, you can place parts of the oven air fryer into the dishwasher to be washed (thus cutting down the cleaning process, if you happen to have a dishwasher).

But, do be aware that it takes up more counter space, and takes a larger initial bite out of your wallet. It may also heat up the kitchen more, and if you are in fashion and aesthetic design, it might be disappointing to find out the colors and themes are more limited than basket air fryers.

These are the two main common types of air fryers; however, there are new types of air fryers that are coming to light for you to use and enjoy, most notably, the paddle-type air fryer. This version has a paddle that moves through the basket of your air fryer in order to help circulate hot air in between each piece of food.

This saves you the effort of pulling your food out at a specific time and shaking or stirring it. These can also be noisy, and heat up the space, and are not small and convenient; however, if you are someone looking for convenience, then this is the air fryer to go for.

Accessory Tools for Air Fryer Cooking

I love how air fryers save time, so I've compiled a list of my favorite time-saving tools that I often use when meal prepping with my air fryer. Anything to help make your life easier and healthier should certainly be considered, and what better way to help than by adding some accessories to your air fryer inventory?

Mandoline

Preparation is always needed before jumping into air frying, and getting yourself the mandoline slicer is the perfect tool to slice online rings, pickles, or even the best and crunchiest chips. You can select the thickness or thinness, depending on what the recipe needs and says, so you will always be able to get the perfect crispness.

Grill Pan

This is simply a pan created with a perforated surface. With this tool, you can both grill and sear foods like fish or even vegetables inside your air fryer. They are also commonly non-stick, which really helps your overall cleanup.

However, before you purchase a grill pan, make sure the air fryer model you have does support the grill pan. The last thing you want is to find that your grill pan just does not fit inside your air fryer.

Heat Resistant Tongs

There is no denying how hot an air fryer can get inside, and unless you are a superhero, you will need some help maneuvering in foods in and outside of the basket if need be. Using heat-resistant tongs can really make your life infinitely easier by keeping your foods, and your hands, safe. They are affordable, and really useful to allow for an even cooking process.

Air Fryer Liners

If you'd like to further decrease your clean-up time, then this is for you! These liners are both non-stick and non-toxic, making this a classic little investment for you to consider. They prevent the food from sticking to your air fryer and help in the process of keeping your little machine clean. You will not have to worry about burnt foods inside your fryer again!

Air Fryer Rack

This adds a little bit more versatility as you can really take advantage of the surface cooking. With a rack, you ensure that heat is evenly distributed to all 360 degrees of your food. They are very safe and easy to use, and they increase the number of dishes you can cook at the same time

Baking Pans

With an air fryer, you can even bake! You just need the right equipment, such as a barrel or round pan. With this you can even bake pizza, bread, muffins, and more. Imagine telling people you baked your own cake with an air fryer!

Silicone Baking Cups

From egg bites to muffins, these are individual cups you can use in order to help compensate for the smaller space within an air fryer. The silicone material is heat-resistant, and allows for easier release of the contents, which spares you a lot of time cleaning. If you are a fan of baking, then this is a must have.

Oil Sprayer

Naturally, one of the top benefits is needing much less oil when cooking with an air fryer, but it does not necessarily mean that you can cook with no oil at all. An oil sprayer is the key to getting the food you want to that nice golden-brown. You can use any oil that you like to use when cooking; all you need is a little spritz before you close the machine, and you are set!

Thermapen

Having the right cooking time is very important, but temperature also counts for a lot, and this is a nice little accessory to add to your collection. Having an instant-read thermometer can ensure all the food you have is cooked (and evenly so). If you are not completely certain at what temperatures food should be, you can always check out the various different guides.

How To Clean An Air Fryer

As mentioned before, an air fryer is really easy to clean, but that doesn't mean you'll never need to clean it! Also, please remember that the cleanliness of your machine depends on how often you use it, and what you use it for.

It is recommended that you clean your air fryer after every use. As tempting as it may be to skip a day, it really is not worth it over the long run. And that is the first step that comes with cleaning an air fryer:

- Do not delay the cleaning. Simply don't. Allowing crumbs or random bits of food to harden overnight can turn an easy task into a nightmare of a chore. If you do happen to air-fry foods that come with a form of sticky sauce, then the warmer they are, the easier again they will be to clean and remove.

- Unplug the machine, and use warm and soapy water to properly remove the dirt and components. You do not want anything abrasive in there. If there is

food that gets stuck, try soaking it until it is soft enough to remove.

- If there is any food that happens to be stuck on the grate or in the basket, then you should consider gently using a toothpick or even a wooden skewer to scrape it off, in order to be thorough with your cleaning process.

- Remember to wipe the inside with a damp, soapy cloth, and remember to remove both the drawer and the basket.

- Finally, wipe the outside of your air fryer with a damp cloth or a sponge.

If there are any odors that seem to be stuck to your air fryer after cooking a strong food, even after you have cleaned it, then you can consider using a product called NewAir.

Just soak it in with water for about 30 minutes to an hour before you clean it. If the smell remains, then rub one lemon half over the drawer and the basket. Allow it to soak for another 30 minutes before washing it again.

Please do be careful with any non-stick appliances. They are a wonder for cleaning, but they can flake or come off over time. Be gentle, as you do not want anything to scratch or to even chip the coating. Not only does it ruin a little bit of the aesthetic look, a small part of your air fryer will constantly be struggling with sticky food.

There you have it! The first stepping stones and foundational knowledge of an air fryer. The device you will choose, and how you will use it is up to you, but there are still so many exciting varieties, choices, and options to come!

Lemon-Blueberry Muffins

Prep T: 5 min | Cook T: 25 min | Servings: 6

Ingredients

- 350 g almond flour
- 3 tbsp Swerve
- 1tsp baking powder
- 2 large eggs
- 3 tbsp melted butter
- 1tbsp almond milk
- 1 tbsp fresh lemon juice
- 64 g fresh blueberries

Directions

1. Preheat the air fryer to 350 F (177 C). Lightly coat 6 silicone muffin cups with vegetable oil. Set aside.
2. In a bowl, merge the almond flour, Swerve, and baking soda. Set aside.
3. In a separate bowl, merge together the eggs, butter, milk, and lemon juice. Attach the egg mixture to the flour mixture and stir until just combined. Roll in the blueberries and let the batter sit for 5 min.
4. Set the muffin batter into the muffin cups, about two-thirds full. Air fry for 20 to 25 min, or until a toothpick inserted into the center of a muffin comes out clean.
5. Detach the basket from the device and let the muffins cool for about 5.

Nutrition: Calories: 165; Fat: 11g; Carbs: 8g; Net Carbs: 7g; Fiber: 1g;

Pancake Cake

Prep T: 10 min | Cook T: 7 min | Servings: 4

Ingredients

- 64 g finely ground almond flour
- 32 g powdered Erythritol
- 1/2 tsp baking powder
- 2 tbsp unsalted butter, softened
- 1 large egg
- 1/2 tsp unflavored gelatine
- 1/2 tsp vanilla extract
- 1/2 tsp ground cinnamon

Directions

1. In a large bowl, merge almond flour, Erythritol, and baking powder. Add butter, egg, gelatine, vanilla, and cinnamon. Pour into 6" round baking pan.
2. Place pan into the air fryer basket.
3. Set the temperature to 149 C/300 F and set the timer for 7 min.
4. When the cake is completely cooked, a toothpick will come out clean. Cut cake into four and serve.

Nutrition: Calories: 153; Protein: 5.4 g; Fiber: 1.7 g; Fat: 13.4 g; Carbohydrates: 12.6 g; Sugar: 9.6 g;

Cheesy Cauliflower Hash Browns

Prep T: 20 min | Cook T: 12 min | Servings: 4

Ingredients

- 340 g steamer bag cauliflower

- 1 large egg
- 128 g shredded sharp Cheddar cheese

Directions

1. After reading the instructions, put the bag in the microwave and cook. Allow it to cool completely and put the cauliflower into a cheesecloth or a kitchen towel and squeeze to remove excess moisture.
2. Pulse cauliflower with a fork and add egg and cheese.
3. Divide a piece of parchment to fit your air fryer basket. Set 1/4 of the mixture, form it into a hash brown patty shape. Now place it onto the parchment and into the air fryer basket, working in batches if necessary.
4. Set the temperature to 204 C/400 F and set the timer for 12 min.
5. Flip the hash browns halfway through the cooking time. Now notice, when completely cooked, they will be golden brown. Serve immediately.

Nutrition: Calories: 153; Protein: 10.3 g; Fiber: 1.7 g; Fat: 9.2 g; Carbohydrates: 4.7 g; Sugar: 1.8 g;

Cauliflower Avocado Toast

Prep T: 15 min | Cook T: 8 min | Servings: 2

Ingredients

- 1 steamer bag cauliflower (340 g)
- 1 large egg
- 64 g shredded mozzarella cheese
- 1 ripe medium avocado
- 1/2 tsp garlic powder
- 1/4 tsp ground black pepper

Directions

1. After reading the directions on the package, cook the cauliflower. To remove excess moisture, remove from bag and place in a clean towel.
2. Place now the cauliflower into a large bowl and mix in egg and mozzarella. Divide a piece of parchment to fit your air fryer basket. Divide the cauliflower into two parts and place them on the parchment. Now shape the two mounds of cauliflower into a 1/4"-thick rectangle. Now place the parchment into the air fryer basket.

3. Set the temperature to 204 C/400 F and set the timer for 8 min.
4. Turn over the cauliflower halfway through the cooking time.
5. When the cooking is over remove the parchment and allow the cauliflower to cool 5 min.
6. Divide open the avocado and remove the pit. Now scoop out the inside, place it in a medium bowl, and mash it with garlic powder and pepper. Now spread onto the cauliflower. Serve immediately.

Nutrition: Calories: 278; Protein: 14.1 g; Fiber: 8.2 g; Fat: 15.6 g; Carbohydrates: 15.9 g; Sugar: 3.9 g;

Walnut Pancake

Prep T: 10 min | Cook T: 20 min | Serving: 4

Ingredients

- 3 tbsp melted butter, divided
- 128 g flour
- 2 tbsp sugar
- 1½ tsp baking powder
- ¼ tsp salt
- 1 egg, beaten
- 96 ml milk
- 1 tsp pure vanilla extract
- 64 g roughly chopped walnuts
- Maple syrup or fresh sliced fruit, for serving

Directions

1. Grease a baking pan with 1 tbsp of melted butter.
2. Mix together the flour, sugar, baking powder, and salt in a medium bowl. Add the beaten egg, the remaining 2 tbsp of melted

butter, milk, and vanilla and stir until the batter is sticky but slightly lumpy.

3. Slowly pour the batter into the greased baking pan and scatter with the walnuts.
4. Place the pan on the bake position.
5. Select Bake, set temperature to 330°F (166°C) and set time to 20 min.
6. When cooked, the pancake should be golden brown and well cooked.
7. Let the pancake rest for 5 min and serve topped with the maple syrup or fresh fruit, if desired.

Nutrition: Calories 271; Fat 14.5 g; Carbohydrates 22 g; Sugar 1.2 g; Protein 11 g;

Sausage and Cheese Balls

Prep T: 12 min | Cook T: 12 min | Servings: 16

Ingredients

- 454 g pork breakfast sausage
- 64 g shredded Cheddar cheese
- 28 g full-fat cream cheese, softened
- 1 large egg

Directions

1. Mix all ingredients in a large bowl. Form into sixteen (2.5 cm) balls. Move the balls into the air fryer basket.
2. Set the temperature to 400 F (204 C) and air fry for 12 min.
3. Shake the basket two- or three-times during cooking. Sausage balls will now be browned on the outside and they will have an internal temperature of at least 145 F (63 C) when completely cooked.
4. Serve warm.

Nutrition: Calories: 424 ; Fat: 32g; Protein: 23g; Carbs: 2g; Fiber: 0g;

Cheesy Bell Pepper Eggs

Prep T: 10 min | Cook T: 15 min | Servings: 4

Ingredients

- 4 medium green bell peppers
- 85 g cooked ham, chopped
- 1/4 medium onion, peeled and chopped
- 8 large eggs
- 128 g mild Cheddar cheese

Directions

1. Cut the tops off each bell pepper. Now remove the seeds and the white membranes with a small knife. After that fill each pepper with ham and onion.
2. Crack 2 eggs into each pepper. Top with 32 g of cheese per pepper. Place into the air fryer basket.
3. Set the temperature to 390 F (199 C) and air fry for 15 min.
4. When fully cooked, peppers will be tender and eggs will be firm. Serve immediately.

Nutrition: Calories: 314 ; Fat: 18g; Protein: 25g; Carbs: 6g; Fiber: 2g;

Bacon-and-Eggs Avocado

Prep T: 5 min | Cook T: 17 min | Servings: 1

Ingredients

- 1 large egg
- 1 avocado, halved, peeled, and pitted
- slices bacon
- Fresh parsley, for serving (optional)
- Sea salt flakes, for garnish (optional)

Directions

1. Set the air fryer basket with avocado oil. Preheat the air fryer to 320 F (160 C). Fill a small bowl with cool water.
2. Soft-boil the egg: Place the egg in the air fryer basket. Air fry for 6 min for a soft yolk or 7 min for a cooked yolk. Bring the egg to the bowl of cool water and let sit for 2 min. Peel and set aside.
3. Use a spoon to carve out extra space in the center of the avocado halves until the cavities are big enough to fit the soft-boiled egg. Place the soft-boiled egg in the center of one half of the avocado and replace the other half of the avocado on top, so the avocado appears whole on the outside.
4. Starting at one end of the avocado, wrap the bacon around the avocado to completely cover it.
5. Place the bacon-wrapped avocado in the air fryer basket and air fry for 5 min. Flip the avocado over and air fry for another 5 min or until the bacon is cooked to your liking.

Serve on a bed of fresh parsley, if desired, and sprinkle with salt flakes, if desired.

6. Best served fresh.

Nutrition: Calories: 536 ; Fat: 46g; Protein: 18g; Carbs: 18g; Fiber: 14g;

Breakfast Cobbler

Prep T: 20 min | Cook T: 30 min | Servings: 4

Ingredients

Filling:
- 283 g bulk pork sausage, crumbled
- 32 g minced onions
- 2 cloves garlic, minced
- 1/2 tsp fine sea salt
- 1/2 tsp ground black pepper
- 1(227-g) package cream cheese (or Kite Hill brand cream cheese style spread for dairy-free), softened
- 187.5 ml beef or chicken broth

Biscuits:
- 3large egg whites
- 96 g blanched almond flour
- 1 tsp baking powder
- 1/4 tsp fine sea salt
- 130 g very cold unsalted butter, cut into 6.5 mm pieces
- Fresh thyme leaves, for garnish

Directions

1. Preheat the air fryer to 400 F (204 C).
2. Place the sausage, onions, and garlic in a pie pan. Using your hands, break up the sausage into small pieces and spread it evenly throughout the pie pan. Season with the salt and pepper. Set the pan in the device and bake for 5 min.
3. While the sausage cooks, place the cream cheese and broth in a food processor or blender and purée until smooth.
4. Detach the pork from the air fryer and use a fork or metal spatula to crumble it more. Pour the cream cheese mixture into the sausage and stir to combine. Set aside.
5. Make the biscuits: Place the egg whites in a medium-sized mixing bowl or the bowl of a stand mixer and whip with a hand mixer or stand mixer until stiff peaks form.

6. In a separate medium-sized bowl, merge together the almond flour, baking powder, and salt, and then cut in the butter. When processed, the mixture should still have chunks of butter. Flip the flour mixture into the egg whites with a rubber spatula.
7. Spoon the dough into 4 equal-sized biscuits, making sure the butter is evenly distributed. Place the biscuits on top of the sausage and cook in the air fryer for 5 min.

Nutrition: Calories: 623 ; Fat: 55g; Protein: 23g; Carbs: 8g; Fiber: 3g;

Nutty Granola

Prep T: 5 min | Cook T: 1 hour | Servings: 4

Ingredients

- 64 g pecans, coarsely chopped
- 64 g walnuts or almonds, chopped
- 32 g unsweetened flaked coconut
- 32 g almond flour
- 32 g flaxseed or chia seeds
- 2 tbsp sunflower seeds
- 2 tbsp melted butter
- 32 g Swerve
- 1/2 tsp ground cinnamon
- 1/2 tsp vanilla extract
- 1/4 tsp ground nutmeg
- 1/4 tsp salt
- 2 tbsp water

Directions

1. Preheat the air fryer to 250F (121C). Divide a piece of parchment paper to fit inside the air fryer basket.
2. In a large bowl, toss all the ingredients until thoroughly combined.
3. Spread now the granola on the parchment paper and flatten to an even thickness.
4. Air fry for 50-60 min, or until golden throughout. Detach from the air fryer and allow to fully cool. Now break the granola into bite-size pieces and store in a covered container for up to a week.

Nutrition: Calories: 305 ; Fat: 28g; Protein: 8g; Carbs: 10g; Fiber: 6g;

BLT Breakfast Wrap

Prep T: 5 min | Cook T: 10 min | Servings: 4

Ingredients

- 227 g reduced-sodium bacon
- 8 tbsp mayonnaise
- 8 large romaine lettuce leaves
- 4 Roma tomatoes, sliced
- Salt and ground black pepper, to taste

Directions

1. Set the bacon in a single layer in the air fryer basket. (It's OK if the bacon sits a bit on the sides.) Set the air fryer to 350F (177C) and air fry for 10 min. Check for crispiness and air fry for 2 to 3 min longer if needed. Cook in batches, if necessary, and drain the grease in between sets.
2. Scatter 1 tbsp of mayonnaise on each of the lettuce leaves and top with the tomatoes and cooked bacon. Flavor to taste with salt and freshly ground black pepper. Roll the lettuce leaves as you would a burrito, securing with a toothpick if desired.

Nutrition: Calories: 370 Fat: 34g; Protein: 11g Carbs: 7g; Fiber: 3g;

Tofu Scramble

Prep T: 5 min | Cook T: 30 min | Servings: 4

Ingredients

- 2 tbsp soy sauce
- 1 tofu block, cubed
- 1 tsp turmeric, ground
- 1 tbsp extra virgin olive oil
- 256 g broccoli florets
- 1/2 tsp onion powder
- 1/2 tsp garlic powder
- 320 g red potatoes, cubed
- 64 g yellow onion, chopped
- Salt and black pepper

Directions

1. Merge tofu with 1 tbsp oil, salt, pepper, soy sauce, garlic powder, onion powder, turmeric and onion in a bowl, stir and leave aside.
2. In a separate bowl, merge potatoes with the rest of the oil, a pinch of salt and pepper and toss to coat.
3. Set potatoes in your air fryer at 177 C/350 F and bake for 15 min, shaking once.
4. Add tofu and its marinade to your air fryer and bake for 15 min.
5. Attach broccoli to the fryer and cook everything for 5 min more.
6. Serve right away.

Nutrition: Calories 140; Fat 4; Fiber 3; Carbs 10; Protein 14;

Swiss chard and Sausage

Prep T: 33 min | Cook T: 20 min | Servings: 8

Ingredients

- 3 eggs
- onion, chopped (64 g)
- olive oil (1 tbsp)
- Swiss chard, chopped (1 Kg)
- black pepper and salt
- 1 garlic clove, minced
- sausage, chopped (454 g)
- mozzarella, shredded (128 g)
- A pinch of nutmeg
- ricotta cheese (256 g)
- parmesan, grated (32 g)

Directions

1. Heat a pan that matches your air fryer with the oil above-average temperature.
2. Add garlic, onions, salt, pepper, nutmeg, and Swiss chard, stir well, cook for around 2 min and take off the heat.
3. Whisk eggs with parmesan, ricotta, and mozzarella cheese in a bowl, stir, and then pour above the Swiss chard mix, stir to mix, include the in your air fryer and cook for around 17 min at 320F.
4. Distribute among plates and serve them.
5. Enjoy!

Nutrition: Calories 332; Fat 13 g; Carbohydrates 14 g; Sugar 2 g; Protein 23 g;

Asparagus Frittata

Prep T: 10 min | Cook T: 5 min | Servings: 2

Ingredients

- 4 eggs, whisked
- 2 tbsp parmesan, grated
- 4 tbsp milk
- Salt and black pepper to the taste
- 10 asparagus tips, steamed
- Cooking Spray

Directions

1. In a bowl, mix eggs with parmesan, milk, salt and pepper and whisk well.
2. Heat up your air fryer at 204 C/400 F and grease with cooking spray.
3. Add asparagus, add eggs mix, toss a bit and cook for 5 min.
4. Divide frittata on plates and serve for breakfast.
5. Enjoy!

Nutrition: Calories 156; Fat 2.5 g; Fiber 4 g; Carbs 7 g; Protein 1g ;

Breakfast Veggie Mix

Prep T: 10 min | Cook T: 25 min | Servings: 6

Ingredients

- 1 yellow onion,
- 1 red bell pepper,
- 1 gold potato,
- 2 tbsp olive oil
- 227 g brie
- 340 g sourdough bread
- 114 g parmesan
- 8 eggs
- 2 tbsp mustard
- 384 ml milk
- Salt and black pepper to the taste

Directions

1. Set up your air fryer at 177 C/350 F, add oil, onion, potato and bell pepper and cook for 5 min.
2. In a bowl, merge eggs with milk, salt, pepper and mustard and whisk well.
3. Attach bread and brie to your air fryer, add half of the eggs mix and add half of the parmesan as well.
4. Add the rest of the bread and parmesan, toss just a little bit and cook for 20 min.
5. Divide among plates and serve for breakfast.
6. Enjoy!

Nutrition: Calories 231; Fat 5; Fiber 10; Carbs 20; Protein 12;

Spinach Zucchini Casserole

Prep T: 10 min | Cook T: 40 min | Servings: 10

Ingredients

- 2 egg whites
- 2 tsp. garlic powder
- 1/2 tsp. pepper
- 32 g parmesan cheese, grated
- 2 small yellow squash, diced
- 64 g breadcrumbs
- 1 tsp. dried basil
- 2 small zucchini, diced
- 32 g feta cheese, crumbled
- 385 g baby spinach
- 1 tbsp. olive oil
- 1/2 tsp. kosher salt

Directions

1. Spray in a casserole dish with cooking spray and set aside.
2. Heat oil in a pan over medium heat.
3. Attach zucchini, yellow squash, and spinach and cook until spinach is wilted about 5 min.
4. Transfer zucchini mixture into the mixing bowl. Add remaining ingredients and mix well.
5. Spread mixture into the prepared casserole dish.
6. Select bake mode. Place the temperature to 400 F and the timer for 40 min. Press start.
7. Let the air fryer preheat then insert the pizza rack into shelf position 5.
8. Place casserole dish on the pizza rack and bake.
9. Serve and enjoy.

Nutrition: Calories 109; Fat 5.2 g; Carbohydrates 10.9 g; Sugar 2.6 g; Protein 6.1 g;

Mozzarella Almond Bagels

Prep T: 15 min | Cook T: 14 min | Servings: 6

Ingredients

- 96 g shredded Mozzarella cheese or goat cheese
- 2 tbsp unsalted butter or coconut oil
- 1 large egg, beaten
- 1 tbsp apple cider vinegar
- 128 g blanched almond flour
- 1 tbsp baking powder
- 1/8 tsp fine sea salt
- 11/2 tsps everything bagel seasoning

Directions

1. Make the dough: Put the Mozzarella and butter in a large microwave-safe bowl and microwave for 1 to 2 min. Stir well. Add the egg and vinegar. Using a hand mixer on medium, combine well. Add the almond flour, baking powder, and salt and, using the mixer, combine well.
2. Set a parchment paper on the countertop and place the dough on it. Knead it for about 3 min.
3. Preheat the air fryer to 350F (180C). Spray a baking sheet or pie pan that will fit into your air fryer with avocado oil.
4. Divide the dough into 6 equal portions. Roll 1 portion into a log that is 15 cm long and about 1.3 cm thick. Form the log into a circle and seal the edges together, making a bagel shape.
5. Set the bagels on the greased baking sheet. Spray the bagels with avocado oil and top with everything bagel seasoning, pressing the seasoning into the dough with your hands.
6. Set the bagels in the air fryer and cook for 14 min, or until cooked through and golden brown, flipping after 6 min.
7. Remove the bagels from the air fryer and allow them to cool slightly before slicing them in half and serving.

Nutrition: Calories: 224; Fat: 19g; Protein:12g; Carbs: 4g; Fiber: 2g

Air Fried Tomato Breakfast Quiche

Prep T: 10 min | Cook T: 30 min | Servings: 1

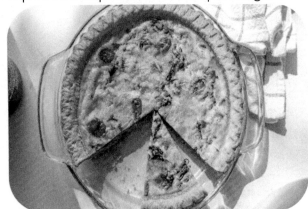

Ingredients

- 2 tbsp yellow onion, chopped
- 2 eggs
- 32 ml milk
- 64 g gouda cheese, shredded
- 32 g tomatoes, chopped
- Salt and black pepper to the taste
- Cooking Spray

Directions

1. Set a ramekin with cooking spray.
2. Crack eggs, add onion, milk, cheese, tomatoes, salt and pepper and stir.
3. Attach this in your air fryer's pan and cook at 171 C/340 F for 30 min.
4. Serve hot.
5. Enjoy!

Nutrition: Calories 239; Fat 6.2; Fiber 8; Carbs 14; Protein 6;

Banana Bread Pudding

Prep T: 10 min | Cook T: 18 min | Serving: 4

Ingredients

- 2 medium ripe bananas, mashed
- 64 ml low-fat milk
- 2 tbsp maple syrup
- 2 tbsp peanut butter
- 1 tsp vanilla extract
- 1 tsp ground cinnamon
- 2 slices of whole-grain bread, torn bite-sized pieces
- 32 g of quick oats
- Cooking Spray

Directions

1. Spritz the sheet pan with cooking spray.
2. In a large bowl, mix the bananas, maple syrup, peanut butter, milk, vanilla extract and cinnamon. You can use an immersion blender to mix until well combined.
3. Stir now in the bread pieces to coat well. Add the oats and stir until everything is combined.
4. Transfer the mixture to the sheet pan. Cover with the aluminium foil.
5. Place the pan on the air fry position.
6. Select Air Fry, set temperature to 375°F (190°C) and set time to 18 min.
7. After 10 min, remove the foil and continue to cook for 8 min.
8. Serve immediately.

Nutrition: Calories 141; Fat 4 g; Carbohydrates 5 g; Sugar 1.2 g; Protein 2 g;

Chicken Meatballs

Prep T: 15 minutes | Cook T: 9 minutes | Servings: 6

Ingredients

- 454 g chicken, minced
- 1 tbsp minced onion
- ¼ tsp minced garlic
- ¼ tsp ground nutmeg
- 1 green bell pepper, diced
- ¼ tsp minced ginger
- ½ tsp salt
- Cooking Spray

Directions

1. Put the minced chicken in the bowl. Add minced onion, garlic, nutmeg, bell pepper, salt, and minced ginger. Stir the ingredients with the help of the spoon until homogenous.
2. Make the chicken balls. Then insert the rack in the air fryer and place the chicken balls inside. Spray them with cooking spray and cook at 204 C/400 F for 9 minutes.
3. Shake the chicken balls after 5 minutes of cooking.

Nutrition: Calories: 122; Fat: 2.4g; Fiber: 0.3g; Carbs: 1.8g; Protein:22.2g

Spiced Pudding

Prep T: 4 minutes | Cook T: 12 minutes | Servings: 2

Ingredients

- ½ tsp cinnamon powder
- ¼ tsp allspice, ground
- 4 tbsp erythritol
- 4 eggs, whisked
- 2 tbsp heavy cream
- Cooking Spray

Directions

1. In a bowl, combine all the ingredients except the cooking spray, whisk well and pour into a ramekin greased with cooking spray. Add the basket to your Air Fryer, put the ramekin inside and cook at 204 C/400 F for 12 minutes.
2. Divide into bowls and serve for breakfast.

Nutrition: Calories: 201; Fat: 11g; Fiber: 2g; Carbs: 4g; Protein:6g

Creamy Chives Muffins

Prep T: 15 minutes | Cook T: 12 minutes | Servings: 4

Ingredients

- 4 slices of ham
- ¼ tsp baking powder
- 4 tbsp coconut flour
- 4 tsps heavy cream
- 1 egg, beaten
- 1 tsp chives, chopped
- 1 tsp olive oil
- ½ tsp white pepper

Directions

1. Preheat the air fryer to 185 C/365 F. Meanwhile, mix up baking powder, coconut flour, heavy cream, egg, chives, and white pepper.
2. Stir the ingredients until getting a smooth mixture. Finely chop the ham and add it in the muffin liquid. Brush the air fryer muffin molds with olive oil. Then pour the muffin batter in the molds. Place the rack in the air fryer basket and place the molds on it.
3. Cook the muffins for 12 minutes (185 C/365 F). Cool the muffins to the room temperature and remove them from the molds.

Nutrition: Calories: 125 ; Fat: 7.8g ; Fiber: 3.5g ; Carbs: 6.1g ; Protein:7.7g

Air Fryer Hot Dogs

Prep/Cook Time 5 min | Servings: 4

Ingredients

- 4 hot dogs
- 4 hot dog buns, sliced down the middle

Directions

1. Preheat air fryer to 400 degrees F.
2. Cook hot dogs for 4 min utes until cooked, moving basket once halfway through to rotate them.
3. Place hot dogs into hot dog buns.
4. Cook hot dogs in buns an additional 1-2 min utes, still at 400 degrees.
5. Enjoy immediately.
6. To air fry frozen hot dogs:
7. Preheat air fryer to 350°F
8. Microwave hot dogs for 30 seconds - 1 minute on defrost (optional)
9. Cook on 350°F for 7-8 min until hot dog is heated thoroughly

Nutrition: Calories 235; Fat 18 g; Carbohydrates 18 g; Protein 10 g;

Smoked Asparagus

Prep T: 5 minutes | Cook T: 20 minutes | Servings: 4

Ingredients

- 454 g asparagus stalks
- Salt and black pepper to the taste
- 32 ml olive oil+ 1 tsp
- 1 tbsp smoked paprika
- tbsp balsamic vinegar

- 1 tbsp lime juice

Directions

1. In a bowl, mix the asparagus with salt, pepper and 1 tsp oil, toss, transfer to your air fryer's basket and cook at 188 C/ 370 F for 20 minutes. Meanwhile, in a bowl, mix all the other ingredients and whisk them well.
2. Divide the asparagus between plates, drizzle the balsamic vinaigrette all over and serve as a side dish.

Nutrition: Calories: 187; Fat: 6g; Fiber: 2g; Carbs: 4g; Protein:9g

Lime and Mozzarella Eggplants

Prep 5 minutes | Cook T: 15 minutes | Servings: 4

Ingredients

- tbsp olive oil
- 2 eggplants, roughly cubed
- 227 g mozzarella cheese, shredded
- 3 spring onions, chopped
- Juice of 1 lime
- 2 tbsp butter, melted
- 4 eggs, whisked

Directions

1. Heat up a pan that fits the air fryer with the oil and the butter over medium-high heat, add the spring onions and the eggplants, stir and cook for 5 minutes.
2. Add the eggs and lime juice and stir well. Sprinkle the cheese on top, introduce the pan in the fryer and cook at 193 C/380 F for 10 minutes.
3. Prepare the portions and serve them as a side dish.

Nutrition: Calories: 212; Fat: 9g; Fiber: 2g; Carbs: 4g; Protein:12g

Green Beans Salad

Prep T: 5 minutes | Cook T: 15 minutes | Servings: 4

Ingredients

- 224 g radishes, chopped
- 226 g green beans, trimmed
- A pinch of salt and black pepper
- 4 eggs, whisked
- Cooking Spray
- 1 tbsp cilantro, chopped

Directions

1. Grease a pan that fits the air fryer with the cooking spray, add all the ingredients, toss and cook at 182 C/360 F for 15 minutes.
2. Divide between plates and serve for breakfast.

Nutrition: Calories: 212; Fat: 12g; Fiber: 3g; Carbs: 4g; Protein:9g

Rosemary Garlic Potatoes

Prep T: 10 min | Cook T: 15 min | Servings: 4

Ingredients

- 512 g baby potatoes, cut into four pieces each
- 2 tsp. dried rosemary, minced
- 3 tbsp. olive oil
- 32 g fresh parsley, chopped
- 1 tbsp. garlic, minced
- 1 tbsp. fresh lemon juice
- Pepper
- Salt

Directions

1. In a large bowl, add potatoes, garlic, rosemary, oil, pepper, and salt and toss well.
2. Spread potatoes in a crispier tray.
3. Place the drip tray below the bottom of the air fryer.
4. Insert the crispier tray into shelf position 4.
5. Select air fry mode. Place the temperature to 400 F and the timer for 15 minutes. Press start.
6. Transfer roasted potatoes in a bowl and toss with parsley and lemon juice.
7. Serve and enjoy.

Nutrition: Calories 148; Fat 10.8 g; Carbohydrates 12.3 g; Sugar 0.1 g; Protein 2.6 g; Cholesterol 0 mg;

Broccoli Salad

Prep and Cook T: 20 min | Serving: 4

Ingredients

- 6 cloves of garlic
- 1 head of broccoli
- Black pepper and salt
- 1 tbsp of Chinese rice wine vinegar
- 1 tbsp of peanut oil

Directions

1. Mix oil, salt, broccoli, and pepper.
2. Place the mixture on the Air Fryer pan.
3. Set the Air Fryer to air fry function.
4. Cook for 9 min at 350 degs F.
5. Place the broccoli in the salad bowl and add peanuts oil, rice vinegar, and garlic.
6. Serve immediately.

Serving Suggestions: toss the broccoli well in

rice vinegar

Prep & Cooking Tips: Separate the broccoli

floret

Nutrition: Calories 157; Fat 14 g; Carbohydrates 5 g; Protein 3 g; Fiber 0 g; Sugar 0 g;

Crispy Cheesy Asparagus

Prep T: 15 min | Cook T: 6 min | Servings: 4

Ingredients

- 2 egg whites
- 32 ml water
- 32 g + 2 tbsp of grated Parmesan cheese, divided
- 96 g panko bread crumbs
- 1/4 tsp salt
- 340 g of fresh asparagus spears, ends trimmed
- Cooking Spray

Directions

1. In a shallow dish, whisk together egg whites, water, until slightly foamy. In a separate shallow dish, thoroughly combine 32 g of Parmesan cheese, breadcrumbs, and salt.
2. Dip now the asparagus in the egg white, then roll in the cheese mixture to coat well.
3. Place the asparagus in the air fry basket in a single layer, leaving space between each spear. Spritz the asparagus with cooking spray.
4. Place the basket on the air fry position.
5. Select Air Fry, set the temperature to 390 F (199 C), and set time to 6 min.
6. When cooking is done, the asparagus should be golden brown, crisp. Remove the basket from the air fryer grill. Sprinkle with the remaining 2 tbsp of cheese and serve hot.

Nutrition: Calories 130; Fat 1.3 g; Carbohydrates 22 g; Protein 6.8 g; Fiber 2.5 g; Sugar 3 g;

Simple Balsamic-Glazed Carrots

Prep T: 5 min | Cook T: 18 min | Servings: 3

Ingredients

- 3 medium-size carrots, cut into 5 cm × 1.2 cm sticks
- 1 tbsp orange juice
- 2 tsps balsamic vinegar
- 1 tsp maple syrup
- 1 tsp avocado oil
- 1/2 tsp dried rosemary
- 1/4 tsp sea salt
- 1/4 tsp lemon zest

Directions

1. Put now the carrots in a baking pan and sprinkle with the balsamic vinegar, orange juice, maple syrup, avocado oil, sea salt, rosemary, finished by the lemon zest. Toss well.
2. Place the pan on the toast position.
3. Select Toast, set temperature to 392 degs F (200 degs C), and set time to 18 min. Stir the carrots several times during cooking.
4. When cooking is done, the carrots should be nicely glazed, tender.

Nutrition: Calories 113; Fat 4.7 g; Carbohydrates 17 g; Protein 1 g; Fiber 3.4 g; Sugar 10 g;

Cabbage and Pork Gyoza

Prep T: 10 min | Cook T: 10 min per batch |

Makes 48 gyozas

Ingredients

- 1 pound (454 g) ground pork
- 1 small head Napa cabbage (1 pound / 454 g), sliced thinly and minced
- 64 g minced scallions
- 1 tsp chopped fresh chives
- 1 tsp soy sauce
- 1 tsp minced fresh ginger
- 1 tbsp minced garlic
- 1 tsp granulated sugar
- 2 tsps kosher salt
- 48 to 50 wonton or dumpling wrappers
- Cooking Spray

Directions

1. To prepare the filling place all the ingredients, except for the wrappers, in a large bowl. Stir to mix well.
2. Unfold a wrapper on a clean work surface, then dab the edges with a little water. Scoop up 2 tsps of the filling mixture in the center.
3. Make the gyoza: Fold the wrapper over to filling and press the edges to seal. Pleat the edges if desired. Repeat with remaining wrappers and fillings.
4. Spritz the crisper tray with cooking spray.
5. Place the crisper tray on the air fry position. Select Air Fry, set the temperature to 360 F (182 C) and set the time to 10 min.
6. Arrange the gyozas in the crisper tray and spritz with cooking spray. Air fry for 10 min or until golden brown. Flip the gyozas halfway through. Work in batches to avoid overcrowding.
7. Serve immediately.

Nutrition: Calories 25; Fat 2 g; Carbohydrates 0.5 g; Protein 1.5 g; Fiber 0 g; Sugar 0 g;

Zucchini and Potato Tots

Prep T: 5 min | Cook T: 20 min | Servings: 4

Ingredients

- 1 large zucchini, grated
- 1 medium baked potato, skin removed and mashed
- 32 g shredded Cheddar cheese
- 1 large egg, beaten
- 1/2 tsp kosher salt
- Cooking Spray

Directions

1. Place the baking pan on the air fry position. Select Air Fry, set the temperature to 390 F (199 C), and set the time to 10 min.
2. Wrap now the grated zucchini in a paper towel and squeeze out any excess liquid, then combine the zucchini, baked potato, shredded Cheddar cheese, egg, and kosher salt in a large bowl.
3. Spray now the baking pan with cooking spray, then place individual tbsp of the zucchini mixture in the pan. Air fry for 10 min. Repeat this process with the
4. remaining mixture.
5. Remove the tots and allow to cool on a wire rack for 5 min before serving.

Nutrition: Calories 128; Fat 3.5 g; Carbohydrates 17 g; Protein 5.3 g; Fiber 2 g; Sugar 1.5 g;

Fried Chicken Tacos

Prep T: 28 min | Cook T: 10 min | Servings: 4

Ingredients

Chicken
- oil for spraying
- Chicken breast, sliced (454 g)
- onion powder
- Garlic powder (1 tsp.)
- One egg
- Paprika (1 tsp.)
- flour
- Buttermilk (3 Tbsp.)
- black pepper
- Corn starch (3 Tbsp.)
- salt
- Cayenne pepper (1/2 tsp.)

Coleslaw
- coleslaw mix (256 g)
- salt
- Red pepper flakes (1/4 tsp.)
- Water (1 Tbsp.)
- brown sugar
- Apple cider vinegar (2 Tbsp.)

Spicy Mayo
- mayonnaise (32 g)
- salt
- Garlic powder (1 tsp.)
- Buttermilk (1 Tbsp.)
- Tortilla wrappers
- Hot sauce (2 Tbsp.)

Directions

1. Add water, salt red pepper flakes, coleslaw mix, brown sugar and apple cider vinegar in a wide bowl, stir thoroughly; set aside.
2. Next, add hot sauce, garlic powder, buttermilk, mayonnaise, and salt to the other bowl, place aside.
3. Pick the Instant Pot; place it in your air fryer.
4. Set the temperature to 182 C/360 F, and press the start button; preheating will begin.
5. Build an exact position by setting two wide flat pans.
6. Add the buttermilk, salt, egg, and pepper to one of the pans, whisk thoroughly.
7. Add corn starch, paprika, black pepper, flour, garlic powder, salt, cayenne pepper, and onion powder in the other bowl, and stir well.

8. Slice the chicken tenders toward 2.5 cm pieces.
9. Season all pieces with pepper and salt.
10. While the Instant Pot is preheated, discard the tray and gently spray it with oil.
11. Cover your chicken with egg batter, followed by the flour batter, and set it on the tray; tray in the bucket.
12. Close your Air Fryer, cover it, and cook for around 10 min at 182 C/360 F.
13. Decorate the top with spicy mayonnaise and coleslaw.

Nutrition: Calories 375; Fat 15 g; Carbohydrates 31 g; Sugar 3 g; Protein 29 g;

Air Fryer Brussels Sprouts

Prep T: 31 min | Cook T: 5 min | Servings: 5

Ingredients

- 1/4 tsp. salt
- 1 tbsp. balsamic vinegar
- 1 tbsp. olive oil
- 2 C. Brussels sprouts

Directions

1. Cut Brussels sprouts in half lengthwise. Toss with salt, vinegar, and olive oil till coated thoroughly.
2. Add coated sprouts to air fryer, cooking 8-10 min at 205 C/ 400 F. Shake after 5 min of cooking.
3. Brussels sprouts are ready to devour when brown and crisp!

Nutrition: Calories 430; Fat 26.5 g; Carbohydrates 27.1 g; Sugar 0 g; Protein 16.7 g;

Mushroom Cakes

Prep T: 10 minutes | Cook T: 8 minutes | Servings: 4

Ingredients

- 255 g mushrooms, finely chopped
- 32 g coconut flour
- 1 tsp salt
- 1 egg, beaten
- 85 g Cheddar cheese, shredded
- 1 tsp dried parsley
- ½ tsp ground black pepper
- 1 tsp sesame oil
- 30 g spring onion, chopped

Directions

1. In the mixing bowl mix up chopped mushrooms, coconut flour, salt, egg, dried parsley, ground black pepper, and minced onion. Stir the mixture until smooth and add Cheddar cheese. Stir it with the help of the fork, Preheat the air fryer to 385F. Line the air fryer pan with baking paper.
2. With the help of the spoon make the medium size patties and put them in the pan. Sprinkle the patties with sesame oil and cook for 4 minutes from each side.

Nutrition: Calories: 164; Fat: 10.7g; Fiber: 3.9g; Carbs: 7.8g; Protein:10.3g

Cheesy Broccoli with Bacon

Prep T: 10 min | Cook T: 10 min | Servings: 2

Ingredients

- 385 g fresh broccoli florets
- 1 tbsp coconut oil
- 64 g shredded sharp Cheddar cheese
- 32 g full Fat sour cream
- 4 slices sugar-free bacon, cooked and crumbled
- 1 scallion, sliced on the bias

Directions

1. Set broccoli into the air fryer basket and drizzle it with coconut oil.
2. Set the temperature to 350 F (180 C) and set the timer for 10 min.
3. Toss now the basket two or three times during cooking to avoid burned spots.
4. You can remove the broccoli when it starts to get crispy at the ends. Top now with shredded cheese, sour cream, and crumbled bacon and garnish with scallion slices.

Nutrition: Calories: 361; Fat: 25g; Protein:18g; Carbs: 11g; Net Carbs: 7g; Fiber: 4g

Asparagus and Green Beans Salad

Prep T: 15 minutes | Cook T: 6 minutes | Servings: 3

Ingredients

- 85 g asparagus, chopped
- 57 g green beans, chopped
- 128 g arugula, chopped
- 1 tbsp hazelnuts, chopped
- 1 tsp flax seeds
- 57 g Mozzarella, chopped
- 1 tbsp olive oil
- ½ tsp salt
- ½ tsp ground paprika
- ½ tsp ground black pepper
- Cooking Spray

Directions

1. Preheat the air fryer to 204 C/400 F. Put the asparagus and green beans in the air fryer and spray them with cooking spray. Cook the vegetables for 6 minutes at 204 C/400 F.

Shake the vegetables after 3 minutes of cooking. Then cool them to the room temperature and put in the salad bowl.
2. Add hazelnuts, flax seeds, chopped Mozzarella, salt, ground paprika, and ground black pepper. Sprinkle the salad with olive oil and shake well.

Nutrition: Calories: 122; Fat: 9.4g; Fiber: 1.9g; Carbs: 4.3g; Protein:6.9g

Mixed Veggies

Prep T: 10 minutes | Cook T: 5 minutes | Servings: 4

Ingredients

- 64 g cauliflower, diced
- 64 g zucchini, diced
- 42.5 g cherry tomatoes, chopped
- 32 g black olives, chopped
- 85 g halloumi cheese, chopped
- 1 tbsp olive oil
- ½ tsp chili flakes
- ½ tsp dried basil
- ½ tsp salt
- Cooking Spray

Directions

1. Put the diced cauliflower in the air fryer pan. Spray them with cooking spray and then add zucchini. Preheat the air fryer to 202 C/395 F and put the pan with vegetables inside it. Cook the vegetables for 5 minutes. Then shake them well and transfer in the salad bowl.
2. Add cherry tomatoes, black olives, chopped halloumi, chili flakes, basil, and salt. Then add olive oil and mix up the anti-pasta.

Nutrition: Calories: 125; Fat: 25.8g; Fiber: 0.9g; Carbs: 2.8g; Protein:5.2g

Lemon and Butter Artichok

Prep T: 5 minutes | Cook T: 15 minutes | Servings: 4

Ingredients

- 340 g artichoke hearts
- Juice of ½ lemon
- 4 tbsp butter, melted

- 2 tbsp tarragon, chopped
- Salt and black pepper to the taste

Directions

1. In a bowl, mix all the ingredients, toss, transfer the artichokes to your air fryer's basket and cook at 188 C/ 370 F for 15 minutes.
2. Prepare the portions and serve them as a side dish.

Nutrition: Calories: 200; Fat: 7g; Fiber: 2g; Carbs: 3g; Protein:7g

Goat Cheese Cauliflower and Bacon

Prep T: 5 minutes | Cook T: 20 minutes | Servings: 4

Ingredients

- 1 Kg cauliflower florets, roughly chopped
- 4 bacon strips, chopped
- Salt and black pepper to the taste
- 64 g spring onions, chopped
- 1 tbsp garlic, minced
- 284 g goat cheese, crumbled
- 32 g soft cream cheese
- Cooking Spray

Directions

1. Grease a baking pan that fits the air fryer with the cooking spray and mix all the ingredients except the goat cheese into the pan.
2. Sprinkle the cheese on top, introduce the pan in the machine and cook at 204 C/400 F for 20 minutes. Prepare the portions and serve them as a side dish.

Nutrition: Calories: 203; Fat: 13g; Fiber: 2g; Carbs: 5g; Protein:9g

Easy French Ratatouille

Prep T: 10 min | Cook T: 12 min | Servings: 6

Ingredients

- 1 medium zucchini, sliced 1.3 cm thick
- 1 small eggplant, peeled and sliced 1.3 cm thick
- 2 tsps kosher salt, divided
- 4 tbsp extra-virgin olive oil, divided
- 3 garlic cloves, minced
- 1 small onion, chopped
- 1 small red bell pepper, cut into 1.3 cm chunks
- 1 small green bell pepper, cut into 1.3 cm chunks
- 1/2 tsp dried oregano
- 1/4 tsp freshly ground black pepper
- 1 pint cherry tomatoes
- 2 tbsp minced fresh basil
- 128 g panko bread crumbs
- 64 g grated Parmesan cheese (optional)

Directions

1. Season one side of the eggplant and zucchini slices with 3/4 tsp of salt. Put the slices, salted side down, on a rack set over a baking sheet. Sprinkle the other sides with 3/4 tsp of salt. Allow to sit for 10 min or until the slices begin to exude water. When ready, rinse and dry them. Cut now the eggplant slices into quarters and the zucchini slices into eighths.
2. Pour the eggplant and zucchini into a large bowl, along with 2 tbsp of olive oil, bell peppers, onion, garlic, oregano, and black pepper. Toss to coat well. Arrange the vegetables on the sheet pan.
3. Place the pan on the toast position.
4. Select Toast, set temperature to 375 degs F (190 degs C), and set time to 12 min.
5. Meanwhile, add basil and tomatoes to the large bowl. Sprinkle with 1 tbsp of olive oil and the remaining 1/2 tsp of salt. Toss well and set aside.
6. Stir together the remaining 1 tbsp of panko, olive oil, and Parmesan cheese (if desired) in a small bowl.
7. After 6 min, remove the pan, add the tomato mixture to the sheet pan, and mix well. Scatter the panko mixture on top. Return the pan to the air fryer grill and continue cooking for 6 min, or until the vegetables are softened, and the topping is golden brown.
8. Cool for 5 min before serving.

Nutrition: Calories 150; Fat 3 g; Carbohydrates 25 g; Protein 4.3 g; Fiber 4.7 g; Sugar 9 g;

Cheesy Greens Sandwich

Prep T: 15 min | Cook T: 10 to 13 min | Servings: 4

Ingredients

- 128 g chopped mixed greens
- 2 garlic cloves, thinly sliced
- 2 tsps olive oil
- 2 slices low-sodium low-fat Swiss cheese
- 4 slices low-sodium whole-wheat bread
- Cooking Spray

Directions

1. Place the baking pan on the air fry position. Select Air Fry, set temperature to 400 F (204 C), and set the time to 5 min.
2. In the baking pan, mix the greens, garlic, and olive oil. Air fry for 4 to 5 min, stirring once until the vegetables are tender. Drain, if necessary.
3. Make 2 sandwiches, dividing half of the greens and 1 slice of Swiss cheese between 2 slices of bread. Lightly spray the outsides of the sandwiches with cooking spray. Transfer to the pan.
4. Bake for 6 to 8 min, turning with tongs halfway through until the bread is toasted and the cheese melts.
5. Cut each sandwich in half and serve.

Nutrition: Calories 160; Fat 9.5 g; Carbohydrates 14 g; Protein 4 g; Fiber 1.2 g; Sugar 1.5 g;

Beet Salad with Parsley Dressing

Prep and Cook T: 30 min |Serving: 4

Ingredients

- Black pepper and salt
- 1 clove of garlic
- 2 tbsp of balsamic vinegar
- 4 beets
- 2 tbsp of capers
- 1 bunch of chopped parsley
- 1 tbsp of olive oil

Directions

1. Place beets on the Air Fryer pan.
2. Set the Air Fryer to air fry function.
3. Set timer and temperature to 15 min and 360 degs F.
4. In another bowl, mix pepper, garlic, capers, salt, and olive oil. Mix well
5. Remove the beets from the Air Fryer and place it on a flat surface.
6. Peel and put it in the salad bowl
7. Serve with vinegar.

Serving Suggestions: Dress with parsley mixture.

Prep & Cooking Tips: rinse beets before cooking.

Nutrition: Calories 66.5; Fat 3 g; Carbohydrates 8 g; Protein 1.2 g; Fiber 2.3 g; Sugar 6 g;

Greek Eggplant Rounds

Prep T: 10 min | Cook T: 10 min | Servings: 4
Ingredients

- 2 tsps olive oil
- 1 long, narrow eggplant, sliced into rounds
- 1/2 tsp salt
- 64 g no-sugar-added marinara sauce
- 64 g feta cheese crumbles
- 8 kalamata olives, pitted and halved
- 2 tbsp chopped fresh dill

Directions

1. Preheat air fryer at 177 C /350 F for 3 min.
2. Rub olive oil over both sides of eggplant circles. Lay out slices on a large plate and season evenly with salt. Top evenly with marinara sauce, feta crumbles, and olives.
3. Place half of eggplant pizzas in ungreased air fryer basket. Cook 5 min. Transfer back to plate. Repeat cooking with remaining pizzas.
4. Garnish with chopped dill and serve warm.

Nutrition: Calories: 82; Protein: 2g; Fiber: 2g; Fat: 5g; Carbohydrates: 7g; Sugar: 4g;

Buddha Bowls

Prep T: 5 min | Cook T: 14 min | Servings: 4
Ingredients

- 1 large carrot, peeled and julienned
- 32 ml apple cider vinegar
- 1/2 tsp ground ginger
- 1/8 tsp cayenne pepper
- 1/2 small yellow onion, peeled sliced into half-moons
- 1 medium parsnip, peeled, sliced

- 1 tsp avocado oil
- 114 g extra-firm tofu, drained and cut into 1/4" cubes
- 1/2 tsp five-spice powder
- 1/2 tsp chili powder
- 2 tsps fresh lime zest
- 128 g fresh arugula
- 64 g steamed rice cauliflower
- 1small avocado, peeled, pitted, and diced
- 2tbsp pine nuts

Directions

1. Preheat air fryer at 177 C/350 F for 3 min.
2. In a small bowl, combine carrot, apple cider vinegar, ginger, and cayenne. Set aside.
3. In a separate small bowl, combine onion, parsnip, and avocado oil. Set aside.
4. In a medium bowl, combine tofu, five-spice powder, and chili powder.
5. Place onion mixture in air fryer basket lightly greased with olive oil. Cook 6 min. Add tofu mixture and toss. Cook an additional 8 min. Stir in lime zest.
6. Prepare Buddha Bowls by evenly distributing arugula, drained carrot juliennes, riced cauliflower, avocado, pine nuts, and tofu mixture between two medium bowls. Serve.

Nutrition: Calories: 183; Protein: 6g; Fiber: 6g; Fat: 13g; Carbohydrates: 14g; Sugar: 4g;

Cheesy Tortillas, Pepper, and Zucchini

Prep T: 5 min | Cook T: 10 min | Servings: 1

Ingredients

- 1 tsp olive oil
- 2 flour tortillas
- 1/4 zucchini, sliced
- 1/4 yellow bell pepper, sliced
- 32 g shredded gouda cheese
- 1 tbsp chopped cilantro
- 1/2 green onion, sliced

Directions

1. Coat the air fry basket with 1 tsp of olive oil.
2. Arrange a flour tortilla in the air fry basket and scatter the top with zucchini, bell pepper, gouda cheese, cilantro, and green onion. Place the other flour tortilla on top.
3. Place the basket on the air fry position.
4. Select Air Fry, set the temperature to 390 F (199 C), and set the time to 10 min.
5. When cooking is complete, the tortillas should be lightly browned, and the vegetables should be tender. Remove from the air fryer grill and cool for 5 min before slicing into wedges.

Nutrition: Calories 394; Fat 21 g; Carbohydrates 40 g; Protein 9 g; Fiber 9 g; Sugar 5 g;

Rosemary Balsamic Glazed Beet

Prep T: 5 min | Cook T: 10 min |Serving: 2

Ingredients

Beet:
- beets, cubed
- tbsp olive oil
- 2 springs rosemary, chopped
- Salt and black pepper, to taste

Balsamic Glaze:
- 42.5 g balsamic vinegar
- 1tbsp honey

Directions

1. Combine the beets, olive oil, rosemary, salt, and pepper in a mixing bowl and toss until the beets are completely coated.
2. Set the beets in the air fryer basket and air fry at 400 F (204 C) for 10 min until the beets are crisp and browned at the edges. Shake now the basket halfway through the cooking time.
3. Meanwhile, make the balsamic glaze: Place the balsamic vinegar and honey in a small saucepan and bring to a boil over medium heat. When sauce starts to boil, reduce the

heat to medium-low heat and simmer until the liquid is reduced by half.

4. When ready, remove the beets from the basket to a platter. Pour the balsamic glaze over the top and serve immediately.

Nutrition: Calories 361; Fat 16.3 g; Carbs 19.3 g; Fiber 0.1 g; Sugar 18.2 g; Protein 33.3 g;

Mexican Topped Avocados

Prep T: 10 min | Cook T: 40 min | Servings: 2

Ingredients

- 128 g seeded and diced tomatoes
- 1 tbsp fresh lime juice
- 1 tsp lime zest
- 2 tbsp chopped fresh cilantro
- 1 small jalapeño, seeded and minced
- 2 cloves garlic, peeled and minced
- 1 tbsp peeled and diced red onion
- 1/2 tsp salt
- 2 large avocados, halved and pitted
- 4 tbsp vegan Cheddar shreds

Directions

1. Combine tomatoes, lime juice, lime zest, cilantro, jalapeño, garlic, onion, and salt in a medium bowl. Cover and refrigerate until ready to use.
2. Preheat air fryer at 177 C/350 F for 3 min.
3. Place avocado halves, cut sides up, in ungreased air fryer. Distribute cheese shreds to top of avocado halves. Cook 4 min.
4. Transfer avocados to a large serving plate, garnish with tomato mixture, and serve.

Nutrition: Calories: 172; Protein: 2g; Fiber: 6g; Fat: 14g; Carbohydrates: 12g; Sugar: 2g;

Honey-Glazed Roasted Vegetables

Prep T: 15 min | Cook T: 20 min |Serving: 3

Ingredients

Glaze:

- 2 tbsp raw honey
- 2 tsps minced garlic
- 1/4 tsp dried marjoram
- 1/4 tsp dried basil
- 1/4 tsp dried oregano
- 1/8 tsp dried sage
- 1/8 tsp dried rosemary
- 1/8 tsp dried thyme
- 1/2 tsp salt
- 1/4 tsp ground black pepper

Veggies:

- 3 to 4 medium red potatoes,
- 1small zucchini, cut into 2.5 to 5 cm pieces
- 1 small carrot, sliced into 6.5 mm rounds
- 1 (298-g) package cherry tomatoes, halved
- 128 g sliced mushrooms
- 2tbsp olive oil

Directions

1. Combine the honey, garlic, marjoram, basil, oregano, sage, rosemary, thyme, salt, and pepper in a small bowl and stir to mix well. Set aside.
2. Place the red potatoes, zucchini, carrot, cherry tomatoes, and mushroom in a large bowl. Whisk with the olive oil and toss to coat.
3. Pour the veggies into the air fryer basket and roast at 380°F (193°C) for 15 min, shaking the basket halfway through.
4. When ready, transfer the roasted veggies to the large bowl. Pour the honey mixture over the veggies, tossing to coat.
5. Spread out the veggies in a baking pan and place in the air fryer.
6. Increase the temperature to 390 F (199 C) and roast for an additional 5 min , or until the veggies are tender and glazed. Serve warm.

Nutrition: Calories: 422; Fat: 19g; Protein: 38g; Sugar: 2g;

Golden Vegetarian Meatballs

Prep T: 15 min | Cook T: 18 min |Serving: 3

Ingredients

- 64 g grated carrots
- 64 g sweet onions
- 2 tbsp olive oil
- 256 g rolled oats
- 64 g roasted cashews
- 256 g cooked chickpeas
- Juice of 1 lemon
- 2tbsp soy sauce
- 1 tbsp flax meal
- 1 tsp garlic powder
- 1 tsp cumin
- 1/2 tsp turmeric

Directions

1. Mix together the carrots, onions, and olive oil in a baking dish and stir to combine.
2. Place now the baking dish in the air fryer basket and roast at 350F (177C) for 6 min.
3. Meanwhile, put oats and cashews in a food processor or blender and pulse until coarsely ground. Transfer the mixture to a large bowl. Add the chickpeas, lemon juice, and soy sauce to the food processor and pulse until smooth. Transfer now the chickpea mixture to the bowl of oat and cashew mixture.
4. Remove the carrots and onions from the basket to the bowl of chickpea mixture. Add the flax meal, garlic powder, cumin, and turmeric and stir to incorporate.
5. Scoop tbsp-sized portions of the veggie mixture and roll them into balls with your hands. Transfer the balls to the air fryer basket in a single layer.
6. Increase the temperature to 370F (188C) and bake for 12 min until golden through. Flip now the balls halfway through the cooking time.
7. Serve warm.

Nutrition: Calories: 527; Carbs: 59.0g; Protein: 21.0g; Fat: 23.0g;

Spicy Kale Chips

Prep T: 5 min | Cook T: 8 to 12 min | Servings: 4

Ingredients

- 640 g kale, large stems removed and chopped
- 2 tsps canola oil
- 1/4 tsp smoked paprika
- 1/4 tsp kosher salt
- Cooking Spray

Directions

1. Place the crisper tray on the air fry position. Select Air Fry, set the temperature to 390 F (199 C), and set the time to 6 min.
2. In a large bowl, toss the kale, canola oil, smoked paprika, and kosher salt.
3. Spray the crisper tray with cooking spray, then place half the kale in the crisper tray. Air fry for 2 to 3 min.
4. Shake the crisper tray and air fry for 2 to 3 more min, or until crispy. Repeat this process with the remaining kale.
5. Remove the kale and allow to cool on a wire rack for 3 to 5 min before serving.

Nutrition: Calories 71.5; Fat 7 g; Carbohydrates 2 g; Protein 0.7 g; Fiber 0.5 g; Sugar 0.3 g;

Avocado Fries with Lime Dipping Sauce

Prep T: 10 min | Cook T: 15 min | Servings: 6

Ingredients

- 227 g of 2 thin, peeled, pitted avocados and cut into 16 wedges
- 1 big egg, beaten lightly
- 96 g of Gluten-free panko breadcrumbs,
- 1 1/4 tsps of lime chili, such as Tajin Classic seasoning salt
- For the sauce for lime dipping
- 32 g of 0 percent Greek Yogurt
- 3 tbsp of mayonnaise light
- Two new tsps of lime juice
- 1/2 tsp of seasoning salt for lime chili, such as Tajin Classic
- 1/8 kosher salt tsp

Directions

1. Preheat the air-fryer to 199 C/390 F
2. Place the egg in a bowl that is shallow. Combine panko with 1 tsp Tajin on another plate.
3. Season the wedges of avocado with 1/4 tsp Tajin. Dip each bit into the egg first and then into the panko.
4. Spray with oil on both sides, and then move to the air fryer and cook halfway for 7 to 8 min. Serve hot with sauce for dipping.

Nutrition: Calories 178; Fat 8 g; Carbohydrates 23 g; Sugar 1 g; Protein 4 g;

Eggplant Bake

Prep T: 3 min | Cook T: 30 min | Servings: 4

Ingredients

- 227 g Cherry tomatoes; cubed
- 64 g cilantro; chopped.
- Four garlic cloves; minced
- Two eggplants; cubed
- One hot chili pepper; chopped.
- Four spring onions; chopped.
- 2tsp. Olive oil
- Salt and black pepper

Directions

1. Grease a baking pan that fits the air fryer with the oil and mix all the pan ingredients.
2. Put the pan in the preheated air fryer and cook for 20 min, divide into bowls and serve.

Nutrition: Calories 232; Fat 12 g; Carbohydrates 5 g; Sugar 0 g; Protein 10 g;

Chapter 4: Poultry Recipes

Fried Buffalo Chicken Taquitos

Prep T: 15 min | Cook T: 5 to 10 min | Servings: 6

Ingredients

- 227 g fat-free cream cheese, softened
- 16 ml Buffalo sauce
- 256 g shredded cooked chicken
- 12 (18 cm) low-carb flour tortillas
- Olive oil spray

Directions

1. Spray the crisper tray lightly with olive oil spray.
2. Place the crisper tray on the air fry position. Select Air Fry, set temp to 360 F (182 C), and set the time to 10 min.
3. In a very large bowl, mix the cream cheese and Buffalo sauce until well combined.
4. Add the chicken and stir until combined.
5. Place the tortillas on a clean workspace. Spoon 2-3 tbsp of the chicken
6. mixture in a thin line down the center of each tortilla. Roll up the tortillas.
7. Place the tortillas in the crisper tray, seam-side down. Spray the tortillas lightly with olive oil spray. You may, if needed, cook the taquitos in batches.
8. Air fry for 5 to 10 min until golden brown.
9. Serve hot.

Nutrition: Calories 177; Fat 7.7 g; Carbohydrates 16 g; Protein 12 g; Fiber 2 g; Sugar 1 g;

Crumbled Chicken Tenderloins

Prep T: 15 minutes | Cook T: 27 minutes | Servings: 4

Ingredients

- 1 egg
- 64 g breadcrumbs
- 2 tbsp. vegetable oil
- 8 reaches chicken tenderloins

Directions

1. Whisk the egg in a mixing bowl.
2. Mix bread crumbs and oil in a separate bowl until the mixture is crumbly.
3. Dip each chicken tenderloin in egg then in the crumb mixture until well coated.
4. Lay the tenderloins on the crisper tray and place the tray on the pizza rack.
5. Select air fry the Air Fryer and set the temperature at 177 C/350 F for 12 minutes. Press start.
6. Serve and enjoy immediately.

Nutrition: Calories: 253; Fat: 11 g; Carbs: 9.8 g; Sugar: 0 g; Protein:26 g;

Ham and Cheese Stuffed Chicken

Prep T: 5 min | Cook T: 25 min | Servings: 4

Ingredients

- 454 g chicken breasts, skinless, boneless and cut into 4 slices
- 114 g goat cheese, crumbled
- 114 g ham, chopped
- 1 egg
- 32 g all-purpose flour
- 32 g parmesan cheese, grated
- 1/2 tsp onion powder
- 1/2 tsp garlic powder

Directions

1. Flatten the chicken breasts with a mallet.

2. Stuff each piece of chicken with cheese and ham. Roll them up and secure with toothpicks.
3. In a shallow bowl, mix the remaining ingredients until well combined. Dip the chicken rolls into the egg/flour mixture.
4. Place the stuffed chicken in the Air Fryer cooking basket. Cook the stuffed chicken breasts at 204 C/400 F for about 22 min, turning them over halfway through the cooking time.

Nutrition: Calories: 560 ; Fat: 21 g; Carbs: 0.5 g ; Sugar: 0.2 g; Protein:86 g;

Lemon-Pepper Chicken Wings

Prep T: 5 min | Cook T: 24 min | Servings: 10

Ingredients

- 2 pounds (907 g) chicken wing flats and drumettes (about 16 to 20 pieces)
- 1.1/2 tsps kosher salt or 3/4 tsp fine salt
- 1.1/2 tsps baking powder
- 4.1/2 tsps salt-free lemon pepper seasoning

Directions

1. Place the wings in a large bowl.
2. In a tiny bowl, stir the salt, baking powder, and seasoning mix. Sprinkle now the mixture over the wings and toss thoroughly to coat the wings. (This works best with your hands.) If you have time, let the wings sit for 20 to 30 min. Place the wings in the baking pan, making sure they don't crowd each other too much.
3. Place the pan on the air fry position. Select Air Fry, set temperature to 375 degs F (191 degs C), and set time to 24 min.

4. After twelve min, remove the pan from the grill. Using tongs, turn the wings over. Rotate the pan 180 degs and return the pan to the grill to continue cooking.
5. When cooking is done, the wings should be dark golden brown and a bit charred in places. Remove the pan, let cool for before serving.

Nutrition: Calories 171; Fat 11.5 g; Carbohydrates 1.2 g; Protein 15.7 g; Fiber 0 g; Sugar 0 g;

Tender Spicy Chicken

Prep T: 1 hour 15 min | Cook T: 20 min | Servings: 4

Ingredients

- 454 g chicken breasts, boneless, skinless
- 64 g rice wine
- 1 tbsp stone-ground mustard
- 1 tsp garlic, minced
- 1 tsp black peppercorns, whole
- 1 tsp chili powder
- 1/4 tsp of sea salt and more to taste

Directions

1. Place the chicken, wine, mustard, garlic, and whole peppercorns in a ceramic bowl. Seal the bowl and let the chicken marinate for about 3 hours in your refrigerator.
2. Discard the marinade and place the chicken breasts in the Air Fryer cooking basket.
3. Cook the chicken breasts at 193 C/380 F for 12 min , turning them over halfway through the cooking time.
4. Season now the chicken with the chili powder and salt. Serve immediately and enjoy!

Nutrition: Calories 404; Fat 29g; Carbohydrates 36g; Sugars 7g; Protein 24g;

Chicken Coconut Meatballs

Prep T: 10 min | Cook T: 10 min | Servings: 4

Ingredients

- 454 g ground chicken
- 11/2 tsp. sriracha
- 1/2 tbsp. soy sauce
- 1/2 tbsp. hoisin sauce
- 32 g shredded coconut
- 1 tsp. sesame oil
- 64 g fresh cilantro, chopped
- 2green onions, chopped
- Pepper
- Salt

Directions

1. Spray air fryer basket with cooking spray.
2. Attach all ingredients into the large bowl and merge until well combined.
3. Make small balls from meat mixture and set into the air fryer basket.
4. Cook at 177 C/350 F for 10 min. Turn halfway through.
5. Serve and enjoy.

Nutrition: Calories 255; Fat 11 g; Carbohydrates 3 g; Sugar 1 g; Protein 32 g;

Hearty Turkey Burger

Prep T: 5 min | Cook T: 13 min | Servings: 4

Ingredients

- 1 pound (454 g) ground turkey
- 1/2 red onion, minced
- 1 jalapeño pepper, seeded, stemmed, and minced
- 3 tbsp bread crumbs
- 1.1/2 tsps ground cumin
- 1 tsp paprika
- 1/2 tsp cayenne pepper
- 1/2 tsp sea salt
- 1/2 tsp freshly ground black pepper
- 4 burger buns, for serving
- Lettuce, tomato, and cheese, if desired, for serving
- Ketchup and mustard, if desired, for serving

Directions

1. Place the grill plate on the grill position. Select Grill, set the temperature to 400 F (204 C), and set the time to 13 min.
2. Meanwhile, in a large bowl, mix the ground turkey, red onion, jalapeño pepper, breadcrumbs, cumin, paprika, cayenne pepper, salt, and black pepper using your hands. Mix until just combined; be careful not to overwork the burger mixture.
3. Dampen your hands with cool water and form the turkey mixture into four patties.
4. Place the burgers on the grill plate. Grill for 11 min.
5. After 11 min, check the burgers for doneness. Cook T is complete when the internal temperature reaches at least 165 F (74 C) on a food thermometer. If necessary, continue grilling for up to 2 min more.
6. Once the burgers are cooked, place each patty on a bun. Top with your preferred fixings, such as lettuce, tomato, cheese, ketchup, and or mustard.

Nutrition: Calories 298; Fat 9 g; Carbohydrates 25.5 g; Protein 20 g; Fiber 3 g; Sugar 3 g;

Chicken Pita Sandwich

Prep T: 10 min | Cook T: 9 to 11 min | Servings: 4

Ingredients

- 2 of boneless, skinless, chicken breasts, 2.5 cm cubes
- 1 small red onion, sliced
- 1 red bell pepper, sliced
- 42.5 g Italian salad dressing, divided
- 1⁄2 tsp dried thyme
- 4 pita pockets, split
- 256 g torn butter lettuce
- 128 g chopped cherry tomatoes

Directions

1. Place the crisper tray on the bake position. Select Bake, set the temperature to 380 F (193 C), and set the time to 11 min.
2. Place the chicken, onion, and bell pepper in the crisper tray. Drizzle with 1 tbsp of the Italian salad dressing, add the thyme and toss.
3. Bake for 9 to 11 min, or until the chicken is 165 F (74 C) on a food thermometer, stirring once during cooking time.
4. Move the chicken and vegetables to a bowl and toss with the remaining salad
5. dressing.
6. Put together the sandwiches with the pita pockets, butter lettuce, and cherry tomatoes. Serve immediately.

Nutrition: Calories 637; Fat 19 g; Carbohydrates 62 g; Protein 51 g; Fiber 10 g; Sugar 3 g;

Chicken Cheesy Quesadilla in Air Fryer

Prep T: 4 min | Cook T: 7 min | Servings: 4

Ingredients

- Precooked chicken: 128 g, diced
- Tortillas: 2 pieces
- Low-fat cheese: 128 g (shredded)

Directions

1. Spray oil the air basket and place one tortilla in it. Add cooked chicken and cheese on top.
2. Add the second tortilla on top. Put a metal rack on top.
3. Cook for 6 min at 188 C/370 F; flip it halfway through so cooking evenly.
4. Slice and serve with dipping sauce.

Nutrition: Calories: 171; Carbohydrates: 8g; Protein: 15g; Fat: 8g;

Chicken Salad Sandwich

Prep T: 15 min | Cook T: 20 min | Servings: 4

Ingredients

- 454 g chicken breasts, boneless and skinless
- 1 stalks celery, chopped
- 1 carrot, chopped
- 1 small onion, chopped
- 128 g mayonnaise
- Sea salt, ground black pepper, to taste
- 4 sandwich buns

Directions

1. Pat the chicken dry with paper towels. Place the chicken in a lightly oiled cooking basket.
2. Cook the chicken breasts at 193 C/380 F for 12 min, turning them over halfway through the cooking time.
3. Shred the chicken breasts using two forks; transfer it to a salad bowl and add in the celery, carrot, onion, mayo, salt, and pepper.
4. Toss to combine and serve in sandwich buns. Enjoy!

Nutrition: Calories 241; Fat 10 g; Carbohydrates 4 g; Sugar 1 g; Protein 35 g;

Sweet and Spicy Turkey Meatballs

Prep T: 15 min | Cook T: 15 min | Servings: 6

Ingredients

- 1 pound (454 g) lean ground turkey
- 64 g whole-wheat panko bread crumbs
- 1 egg, beaten
- 1 tbsp soy sauce
- 32 g plus 1 tbsp hoisin sauce, divided
- 2 tsps minced garlic
- 1/8 tsp salt
- 1/8 tsp freshly ground black pepper
- 1 tsp sriracha
- Olive oil spray

Directions

1. Spray the crisper tray lightly with olive oil spray.
2. Place the crisper tray on the air fry position. Select Air Fry, set temp to 350 F (177 C), and set the time to 15 min.
3. Get a bowl, mix together the turkey, panko bread crumbs, egg, soy sauce, 1 tbsp of hoisin sauce, garlic, salt, and black pepper.
4. Using a tbsp, form the mixture into 24 meatballs.
5. In a small bowl, combine the remaining 32 g of hoisin sauce and sriracha to make a glaze and set aside.
6. Place the meatballs in the crisper tray in a single layer. You may need to cook them in batches.
7. Air fry for 8 min. Brush now the meatballs generously with the glaze and air fry until cooked through, an additional 4 to 7 min.
8. Serve warm.

Nutrition: Calories 147; Fat 6 g; Carbohydrates 6.5 g; Protein 15 g; Fiber 0.3 g; Sugar 0.5 g;

White Wine Chicken Breast

Prep T: 30 min | Cook T: 28 min | Servings: 4

Ingredients

- 1/2 tsp grated fresh ginger
- 42.5 ml coconut milk
- 1/2 tsp sea salt flakes
- 3 medium-sized boneless chicken breasts, cut into small pieces
- 11/2 tbsp sesame oil
- 3 green garlic stalks, finely chopped
- 64 ml dry white wine
- 1/2 tsp fresh thyme leaves, minced
- 1/3 tsp freshly cracked black pepper

Directions

1. Warm the sesame oil in a deep sauté pan over a moderate heat. Then, sauté the green garlic until just fragrant.
2. Detach the pan from the heat and pour in the coconut milk and the white wine. After that, add the thyme, sea salt, fresh ginger, and freshly cracked black pepper. Scrape this mixture into a baking dish.
3. Stir in the chicken chunks.
4. Cook in the preheated Air Fryer for 28 min at 335F (168C). Serve on individual plates and eat warm.

Nutrition: Calories: 471; Fat: 28g; Protein:12g; Carbs: 31g; Net Carbs: 31g; Fiber: 0g

Baked Chicken Tenders

Prep T and cooking time: 45 min | Servings: 6-8

Ingredients

- 454 g of boneless chicken tenders
- 2 eggs
- 2 tsp. of butter, melted
- 85 g of graham crackers
- 85 g of breadcrumbs

- Barbecue sauce
- Salt and pepper for seasoning

Directions

1. Preheat the Air Fryer to 232 C/450 F and spray some oil on the baking pan
2. Combine the crackers, breadcrumbs, and butter until smooth.
3. Beat the eggs in another bowl with salt and pepper.
4. Dip the chicken pieces in the eggs first and then the breadcrumbs.
5. Bake for 15-18 min.

Nutrition: Calories 147; Fat 6 g; Carbohydrates 6 g; Protein 16.5 g; Fiber 0.2 g; Sugar 0.5 g;

Fast Bacon-Wrapped Chicken Breasts

Prep T: 10 min | Cook T: 15 min | Servings: 4

Ingredients

- 32 g chopped fresh chives
- 2 tbsp lemon juice
- 1 tsp dried sage
- 1 tsp fresh rosemary leaves
- 64 g fresh parsley leaves
- 4 cloves garlic, peeled
- 1 tsp ground fennel
- 3 tsps sea salt
- 1/2 tsp red pepper flakes
- 4 (113-g) skinless, boneless, chicken breasts, pounded 6.5 mm thick
- 8 slices bacon
- Sprigs of fresh rosemary, for garnish
- Cooking Spray

Directions

1. Spritz the air fry basket with cooking spray.
2. Put the chives, garlic, fennel, salt, lemon juice, rosemary, parsley, sage, and red pepper flakes in a food processor, then pulse to purée until smooth.
3. Unfold the chicken breasts on a clean work surface, then brush the top side of the chicken breasts with the sauce.
4. Roll the chicken breasts up from the shorter side, then wrap each chicken rolls with 2 bacon slices to cover. Secure with toothpicks.
5. Arrange the rolls in the air fry basket.
6. Place the basket on the air fry position.
7. Select Air Fry. Set temperature to 340 F (171 C) and set time to 10 min. Flip the rolls halfway through.
8. After 10 min, increase temperature to 390 F (199 C) and set time to 5 min.
9. When the cooking is done, the bacon should be browned and crispy.
10. Transfer the rolls to a large plate. Discard the toothpicks and spread with rosemary sprigs before serving.

Nutrition: Calories 221; Fat 11 g; Carbohydrates 1.25 g; Protein 31 g; Fiber 0.5 g; Sugar 0 g;

Country-Style Turkey Drumsticks

Prep T: 20 min | Cook T: 45 min | Servings: 5

Ingredients

- 907 g turkey drumsticks, bone-in
- 2 tbsp olive oil
- Kosher salt, freshly ground black pepper, to taste
- 1tsp dried thyme
- 1 tsp dried rosemary
- 1 tsp garlic, minced

Directions

1. Toss the turkey drumsticks with the remaining ingredients.
2. Cook the turkey drumsticks at 204 C/400 F for 40 min, turning them over halfway through the cooking time.

Nutrition: Calories: 171 ; Carbs: 8g; Protein:15g ; Fat: 8g

Almond Chicken Curry

Prep T: 10 minutes | Cook T: 15 minutes | Servings: 2

Ingredients

- 284 g chicken fillet, chopped
- 1 tsp ground turmeric
- 64 g spring onions, diced
- 1 tsp salt
- ½ tsp curry powder
- ½ tsp garlic, diced
- ½ tsp ground coriander
- 64 ml of organic almond milk
- 1 tsp Truvia
- 1 tsp olive oil

Directions

1. Put the chicken in the bowl. Add the ground turmeric, salt, curry powder, diced garlic, ground coriander, and almond Truvia. Then add olive oil and mix up the chicken. After this, add almond milk and transfer the chicken in the air fryer pan. Then preheat the air fryer to 191 C/375 F and place the pan with korma curry inside.
2. Top the chicken with diced onion.
3. Cook the meal for 10 minutes. Stir it after 5 minutes of cooking. If the chicken is not cooked after 10 minutes, cook it for an additional 5 minutes.

Nutrition: Calories: 327; Fat: 14.5g; Fiber: 1.5g; Carbs: 5.6g; Protein:42g

Buttermilk Fried Chicken

Prep T: 30 min | Cook T: 25 min | Servings: 4

Ingredients

- 454 g chicken breast halves
- salt and ground black pepper, to taste
- 128 g buttermilk
- 128 g all-purpose flour
- 1/2 tsp onion powder
- 1 tsp garlic powder
- 1 tsp smoked paprika

Directions

1. Toss together the chicken pieces, salt, and black pepper in a large bowl to coat. Stir in the buttermilk until the chicken is coated on all sides. Place the chicken in your refrigerator for about 6 hours.
2. In a shallow bowl, thoroughly combine the flour, onion powder, garlic powder, and smoked paprika.
3. Then, dredge the chicken in the seasoned flour; shake off any excess and transfer them to a lightly oiled Air Fryer basket.
4. Cook the chicken breasts at 193 C/380 F for 12 min, turning them over halfway through the cooking time.
5. Enjoy!

Nutrition: Calories: 271; Proteins 29g; Carbs: 20g; Fat: 15g

Sesame Chicken Thighs

Prep T: 15 minutes | Cook T: 55 minutes | Servings: 4

Ingredients

- 2 tbsp. sesame oil
- 2 tbsp. soy sauce
- 1 tbsp. honey
- 1 tbsp. sriracha sauce
- 1 tbsp. rice vinegar
- 908 g chicken thighs
- 1 green onion, chopped
- 2 tbsp. sesame seeds, toasted

Directions

1. Get yourself a bowl and mix in the first 5 ingredients. Add chicken to the bowl and stir until well coated.
2. Cover and put in the fridge for about 30 minutes.
3. Drain the marinade and place the chicken in the crisper tray. Place the crisp tray on the pizza rack of the Air Fryer.

4. Select the air fry setting and set the temperature at 204 C/400 F for 15 minutes. Press start.
5. When you have cooked for 5 minutes, flip and cook for an additional 10 minutes.
6. Let the chicken rest for 5 minutes before serving.

Nutrition: Calories: 484; Fat: 33 g; Carbs: 6.6 g; Sugar: 0 g; Protein:40 g;

BBQ Cheddar Stuffed Chicken Breasts

Prep T: 15 minutes | Cook T: 35 minutes | Servings: 2

Ingredients

- 3 strips bacon
- 2 (113 g) chicken breast skinless and boneless
- 57 g cheddar cheese, cubed
- 32 g BBQ sauce
- 1 pinch of salt and black pepper

Directions

1. Place 1 strips of bacon in a crisper tray and air fry for 2 minutes. Cut the bacon into small pieces.
2. Line the crisper tray with parchment paper.
3. Make a 2.5 cm cut on the chicken horizontally such that you create an internal pouch.
4. Stuff each chicken breast with cooked bacon and cheese mixture, and then wrap the breasts with bacon.
5. Cover the chicken with BBQ sauce and place them on the lined tray.
6. Set temperature of the Air Fryert to 193 C/380 F and the time for 20 minutes. Press start.
7. Turn the chicken breasts when halfway cooked. The chicken internal temperature should be 165 degs F when fully cooked. Serve.

Nutrition: Calories: 375; Fat: 19 g; Carbs: 12.3 g; Sugar: 0 g; Protein:38 g;

Cajun Grilled Chicken and Pepper Kebabs

Prep T: 75 min | Cook T: 85 min | Servings: 6

Ingredients

- Ground cumin 2 tsp.
- Sunflower oil 4 tbsp.
- Yellow pepper 1, deseeded and cut in 2.5cm pieces, cut into quarters
- Lime juice 2 tbsp.
- Oregano 1 tsp.
- Ground coriander 2 tsp.
- Green pepper 1, deseeded and cut in 2.5cm pieces, cut into quarters
- Paprika 2 tsp.
- Wooden skewers 6, soaked in water for 30 min
- Chicken thighs, cut into 2.5cm cubes 600g
- Chili flakes 1/2 tsp.
- To taste, salt, freshly ground black pepper
- Red pepper 1, deseeded and cut in 2.5cm pieces, cut into quarters
- Small red onions 2, (peeled and cut into 2.5cm pieces)

Directions

1. Combine the oil, cumin, lime juice, coriander, oregano, paprika, chili flakes, pepper, and salt in a bowl to taste. Insert the pieces of chicken and mix to cover them. Cover and allow marinating for at least an hour in the refrigerator.
2. In the machine, insert the grill plate and close the cover. Pick GRILL, set MED to set the temperature and set the time to ten min. To commence preheating, click START/STOP.
3. Gather your skewers in the following manner when the machine is preheating until they are almost full: chicken, onion, and pepper. Ensure that the products are nearly exclusively squeezed down at the bottom of the skewers. Reserve some marinade for shaving.

4. Place kebabs on the grill plate until the machine has beeped to indicate it has preheated. Close the lid
5. Open lid baste uncovered side of the kebabs with marinade when the machine beeps and the screen reads FLIP halfway into cooking. Flip the skewers and baste them again with silicone tongs. To finish cooking, close the lid.
6. When the chicken achieves an internal temp of 75 C, cooking is done. Open the cover and cut the skewers off. On a tray, put the kebabs and serve with rice/salad.

Nutrition: Calories 271; Proteins 29g; Carbs 20g; Fat 15g;

Delicious Chicken Fajitas

Prep T: 10 min | Cook T: 15 min | Servings: 4

Ingredients

- 4 chicken breasts
- 1 onion, sliced
- 1 bell pepper, sliced
- 1 1/2 tbsp. fajita seasoning
- 2 tbsp olive oil
- 96 g cheddar cheese, shredded

Directions

1. Preheat the air fryer at 193 C/380 F.
2. Coat chicken with oil and rub with seasoning.
3. Place chicken into the air fryer baking dish and top with bell peppers and onion.
4. Cook for 15 min.
5. Top with shredded cheese and cook for 1-2 min until cheese is melted.
6. Serve and enjoy.

Nutrition: Calories 425; Fat 23 g; Carbohydrates 7 g; Sugar 2 g; Protein 45 g;

Cheesy Beef Meatballs

Prep T: 5 min | Cook T: 18 min | Servings: 6

Ingredients

- 1 pound (454 g) ground beef
- 64 g grated Parmesan cheese
- 1 tbsp minced garlic
- 64 g Mozzarella cheese
- 1 tsp freshly ground pepper

Directions

1. Place the crisper tray on the air fry position. Select Air Fry, set temp to 400 F (204 C) and set the time to 18 min.
2. Get a bowl and combine all the ingredients in it.
3. Roll the meat mixture into 5 generous meatballs. Transfer to the crisper tray.
4. Air fry for 18 min.
5. Serve immediately.

Nutrition: Calories 176.5; Fat 11.5 g; Carbohydrates 0.2 g; Protein 16.5 g; Fiber 0 g; Sugar 0 g;

Bacon Cheeseburger Casserole

Prep T: 10 min| Cook T: 35 min | Servings: 6

Ingredients

- 1small onion, chopped
- 1 tbsp ground mustard
- 1 tbsp Worcestershire sauce
- 1/2 can (425 g) tomato sauce
- 64 g grape tomatoes, chopped
- 64 g shredded cheddar cheese
- 32 g sliced dill pickles
- 454 g ground beef
- 114 g process cheese (Velveeta)
- 6 bacon strips, cooked and crumbled
- 226 g frozen Tater Tots

Directions

1. Lightly grease baking pan of air fryer with cooking spray. Add beef and half of onions.
2. For 10 min, cook on 199 C/390 F. Halfway through cooking time, stir and crumble beef.
3. Stir in Worcestershire, mustard, Velveeta, and tomato sauce. Mix well. Cook for 4 min until melted.
4. Mix well and evenly spread in pan. Top with cheddar cheese and then bacon strips.
5. Evenly top with tater tots. Cover pan with foil.
6. Cook for 15 min at 199 C/390 F. Uncover and bake for 10 min more until tops are lightly browned.
7. Serve and enjoy topped with pickles and tomatoes and remaining onion.

Nutrition: Calories: 483; Carbs: 24.0g; Protein: 27.0g; Fat: 31.0g;

Lamb and Feta Hamburgers

Prep T: 15 min | Cook T: 16 min | Makes 4 burgers

Ingredients

- 1.1/2 pounds (680 g) ground lamb
- 32 g crumbled feta
- 1.1/2 tsps tomato paste
- 1.1/2 tsps minced garlic

- 1 tsp ground dried ginger
- 1 tsp ground coriander
- ¼ tsp salt
- ¼ tsp cayenne pepper
- 4 kaiser rolls or hamburger buns, split open lengthwise, warmed
- Cooking Spray

Directions

1. Spritz the crisper tray with cooking spray.
2. Place the crisper tray on the air fry position. Then set the temperature to 375 F (191 C) in Air Fry mode and set the time to 16 min.
3. Place all the ingredients, except for the buns, in a large bowl. Coarsely stir to mix well.
4. Shape the mixture into four balls, then pound the balls into four 12 cm diameter patties.
5. Arrange the patties in the crisper tray and spritz with cooking spray. Air fry for 16 min or until well browned. Flip the patties halfway through.
6. Assemble the buns with patties to make the burgers and serve immediately.

Nutrition: Calories 643; Fat 42 g; Carbohydrates 25 g; Protein 29.5 g; Fiber 3.5 g; Sugar 5 g;

Parmesan Crusted Pork Chops

Prep T: 10 min | Cook T: 15 min | Servings: 8
Ingredients

- 3 tbsp. grated parmesan cheese
- 1C. pork rind crumbs
- 2beaten eggs
- 1/4 tsp. chili powder
- 1/2 tsp. onion powder
- 1 tsp. smoked paprika
- 1/4 tsp. pepper
- 1/2 tsp. salt
- 4-6 thick boneless pork chops

Directions

1. Ensure your air fryer is preheated to 205 C/ 400 F.
2. With pepper and salt, season both sides of pork chops.
3. In a food processor, pulse pork rinds into crumbs. Mix crumbs with other seasonings.
4. Beat eggs and add to another bowl.

5. Dip pork chops into eggs then into pork rind crumb mixture.
6. Spray down the air fryer with olive oil and add pork chops to the basket. Set temperature to 204 C/400 F, and set time to 15 min.

Nutrition: Calories: 422; Fat: 19g; Protein:38g; Sugar:2g;

Beef Roast in Worcestershire-Rosemary

Prep T: 10 min| Cook T: 2 hours| Servings: 6
Ingredients

- 1onion, chopped
- 1 tbsp butter
- 1 tbsp Worcestershire sauce
- 1 tsp rosemary
- 1 tsp thyme
- 454 g beef chuck roast
- 2cloves of garlic, minced
- 3tbsp olive oil
- 256 ml water
- 3 stalks of celery, sliced

Directions

1. Preheat the air fryer for 5 min.
2. Set all ingredients in a deep baking dish that will fit in the air fryer.
3. Bake for 2 hours at 177 C/350 F.
4. Braise the meat with its sauce every 30 min until cooked.

Nutrition: Calories: 260Carbohydrates: 2.9gProtein: 17.5gFat: 19.8

Panko-Crusted Beef Steaks

Prep T: 5 min | Cook T: 10 min | Servings: 4

Ingredients

- 4 beef steaks
- 2 tsps caraway seeds
- 2 tsps garlic powder
- Sea salt and cayenne pepper, to taste
- 1 tbsp melted butter
- 42.5 g almond flour
- 2 eggs, beaten

Directions

1. Put now the beef steaks in a large bowl and toss with the garlic powder, caraway seeds, salt, and pepper until well coated.
2. Stir now the melted butter and almond flour in a bowl.
3. Whisk now the eggs in a different bowl.
4. Dredge the seasoned steaks in the eggs, then dip in the almond and butter mixture.
5. Arrange the coated steaks in the air fry basket.
6. Place the basket on the air fry position.
7. Select Air Fry. Set temperature to 355 degs F (179 degs C) and set time to 10 min. To ensure even cooking flip the steaks once halfway through.
8. When cooking is done, the internal temperature of the beef steaks should reach at least 145 degs F (63 degs C) on a meat thermometer.
9. Transfer the steaks to plates. Let cool for 5 min and serve hot.

Nutrition: Calories 311; Fat 11 g; Carbohydrates 0 g; Protein 54 g; Fiber 0 g; Sugar 0 g;

Air-Fried Lamb Chops with Asparagus

Prep T: 10 min | Cook T: 15 min | Servings: 4

Ingredients

- 4 asparagus spears, trimmed
- 2 tbsp olive oil, divided
- 1 pound (454 g) lamb chops
- 1 garlic clove, minced
- 2 tsps chopped fresh thyme for serving
- Salt and ground black pepper, to taste

Directions

1. Spritz the air fry basket with cooking spray.
2. On a large plate, brush the asparagus with 1 tbsp olive oil, then sprinkle with salt. Set aside.
3. On a separate plate, brush the lamb chops with remaining olive oil and sprinkle with ground black pepper and salt.
4. Arrange the lamb chops in the basket.
5. Place the basket on the air fry position.
6. Select Air Fry. Set temperature to 400 F (205 C) and set time to 15 min. Flip the lamb chops and add the asparagus and garlic halfway through.
7. When cooking is done, the lamb should be well browned and the asparagus should be tender.
8. Serve them on a plate with thyme on top.

Nutrition: Calories 270; Fat 21 g; Carbohydrates 0.3 g; Protein 18.5 g; Fiber 0.3 g; Sugar 0 g;

Ginger Pork

Prep T: 10 minutes | Cook T: 20 minutes | Servings: 5

Ingredients

- 453 g pork tenderloin
- 1 tbsp fresh ginger, chopped
- 1 red bell pepper, cut into wedges
- 1 tbsp lemon juice
- 1 tsp Erythritol
- 64 g coconut flour
- ½ tsp salt
- ¼ tsp chili powder
- ½ tsp minced garlic
- 85 g celery stalk
- 2 eggs, beaten
- 32 ml beef broth
- 1 tsp apple cider vinegar
- 1 tbsp butter

Directions

1. Chop the pork tenderloin into medium cubes and sprinkle with salt and chili powder. After this, dip the pork cubes in the beaten egg and coat in the coconut flour.
2. Preheat the air fryer to 204 C/400 F ad put the pork cubes in the air fryer basket. Cook them for 3 minutes. When the time is finished, flip the pork cubes on another side and cook for 3 minutes more.
3. Meanwhile, make the sweet-sour sauce. Put the butter in the pan. Add apple cider vinegar, chopped celery stalk, minced garlic, lemon juice, Erythritol, bell pepper, and fresh finger.
4. Cook the mixture over the medium heat for 6 minutes. Stir the mixture from time to time. Then add beef broth and bring the mixture to boil.
5. Add the cooked pork cubes and cook the meal for 4 minutes more.

Nutrition: Calories: 241; Fat: 8.7g; Fiber: 5.6g; Carbs: 11.5g; Protein:28.3g

Char Siu (Chinese BBQ Pork)

Prep T: 8 hours 10 min | Cook T: 15 min | Servings: 4

Ingredients

- 32 g honey
- 1 tsp Chinese five-spice powder
- 1 tbsp Shaoxing wine (rice cooking wine)
- 1 tbsp hoisin sauce
- 2 tsps minced garlic
- 2 tsps minced fresh ginger
- 2 tbsp soy sauce
- 1 tbsp sugar
- 1 pound (454 g) of fatty pork shoulder, long, 2.5 cm-thick pieces
- Cooking Spray

Directions

1. Put all your ingredients, exception made for the pork shoulder, in a microwave-safe bowl. Stir to mix well. Microwave until the honey has dissolved. Stir periodically.
2. Pierce now the pork pieces generously with the aid of a fork, then put the pork in a large bowl.
3. Pour in half of the honey mixture. Set now your remaining sauce aside until it is ready to serve.
4. Press now your pork pieces into the mixture to coat and wrap the bowl in plastic, then let it rest into the refrigerator to marinate for at least 8 hours.
5. Spritz the air fry basket with cooking spray.
6. Discard now the marinade and transfer the pork pieces in the air fry basket.

7. Place the basket on the air fry position.
8. Select Air Fry. Set temperature to 400 F (205 C) and set time to 15 min. Flip the pork halfway through.
9. When cooking is done, the pork's color should be well browned.
10. Meanwhile, microwave your remaining marinade on high setting for a minute or until it has a thick consistency. Stir periodically.
11. Remove the pork from the air fryer grill and allow to cool for 10 min before serving with the thickened marinade.

Nutrition: Calories 209; Fat 7 g; Carbohydrates 2 g; Protein 32 g; Fiber 0 g; Sugar 1 g;

Curry Pork Roast in Coconut Sauce

Prep T: 25 min | Cook T: 60 min | Servings: 6

Ingredients

- 1/2 tsp curry powder
- 1/2 tsp ground turmeric powder
- 1can unsweetened coconut milk
- 1 tbsp sugar
- 2tbsp fish sauce
- 2tbsp soy sauce
- 1.3 Kg of pork shoulder
- Salt and pepper to taste

Directions

1. Place all ingredients in a bowl and allow the meat to marinate in the fridge for at least 2 hours.
2. Preheat the air fryer to 199 C/390 F.
3. Place the grill pan accessory in the air fryer.
4. Grill the meat for 20 min making sure to flip the pork every 10 min for even grilling and cook in batches.
5. Meanwhile, merge the marinade into a saucepan and allow to simmer for 10 min until the sauce thickens.
6. Baste the pork with the sauce before serving.

Nutrition: Calories: 688; Carbs: 38g; Protein: 17g; Fat: 52g;

Beef Empanada

Prep T: 20 min | Cook T: 20 min | Servings: 2

Ingredients

- 1 tbsp olive oil
- 227 g ground beef
- 1/2 onion, minced
- 1 clove garlic, minced
- 1 green bell pepper, diced
- 32 ml tomato salsa
- Salt and pepper to taste
- 1/4 tsp cumin
- 1 egg yolk
- 1 tbsp milk
- 1 pack empanada shells

Directions

1. Add some oil to a pan over medium heat.
2. Cook the ground beef for 5 min.
3. Drain the fat.
4. Stir in the onion and garlic.
5. Cook for 4 min.
6. Add bell pepper and salsa.
7. Season with salt, pepper and cumin.
8. Cook for 10 min.
9. In a bowl, mix egg yolk and milk.
10. Place ground beef mixture on the top of the empanada shells.
11. Fold and seal.
12. Brush both sides with egg wash.
13. Add empanada to the air fryer.
14. Set it to air fry.
15. Cook it now, 204 C/400 F, 10 min.

<u>Serving Suggestions:</u> Serve with coffee.

<u>Prep & Cooking Tips:</u> Use lean ground beef.

Nutrition: Calories 235; Fat 20 g; Carbohydrates 4 g; Sugar 2.5 g; Protein 27 g;

Air Fried Beef and Mushroom Stroganoff

Prep T: 5 min | Cook T: 14 min | Servings: 4

Ingredients

- 454 g of beef steak, thinly sliced
- 227 g of mushrooms, sliced
- 1 onion, chopped
- 256 ml of beef broth
- 128 g sour cream
- 4 tbsp butter, melted
- 256 g cooked egg noodles

Directions

1. Merge the mushrooms, onion, beef broth, sour cream and butter in a bowl until well blended. Add the beef steak to another bowl.
2. Set the mushroom mixture over the steak and let marinate for 10 min.
3. Set the marinated steak in a baking pan.
4. Select Bake, Convection, set temperature to 400 F (205 C) and set time to 14 min. Press Start to begin preheating.
5. Set the pan on the bake position. Cook the steak halfway through the cooking time.
6. When cooking is processed, the steak should be browned and the vegetables should be tender.
7. Serve hot with the cooked egg noodles.

Nutrition: Calories 282; Fat 14 g; Carbohydrates 0 g; Sugar 0 g; Protein 44 g; Cholesterol 0 mg;

Panko-Crusted Lamb Rack

Prep T: 10 min | Cook T: 20 min | Servings: 2

Ingredients

- 64 g finely chopped pistachios
- 1 tsp chopped fresh rosemary
- 3 tbsp panko bread crumbs
- 2 tsps chopped fresh oregano
- 1 tbsp of olive oil
- Salt, freshly ground black pepper, to taste
- 1 lamb rack, bones fat trimmed, frenched
- 1 tbsp Dijon mustard

Directions

1. Put the oregano, pistachios, rosemary, olive oil, bread crumbs, salt, and black pepper in a food processor. Pulse to combine until smooth.
2. Rub now the lamb rack with the salt and the black pepper on a clean work surface, then place it in the air fry basket.
3. Place the basket on the air fry position.
4. Select Air Fry. Set temperature to 380 F (193 C) and set time to 12 min. Flip the lamb halfway through.
5. When cooking is done, the lamb should be lightly browned.
6. Now take the lamb and place it on a plate. Brush the fat part with mustard and sprinkle the lamb rack with the pistachios mixture to coat well.
7. Put now the lamb rack back to the air fryer grill and air fry for 8 more min or until internal temperature of the rack reaches at least 145 F (63 C).
8. Remove now the lamb rack from the air fryer grill with tongs and allow to cool for 5 min before slicing to serve.

Nutrition: Calories 200; Fat 12 g; Carbohydrates 8 g; Protein 11 g; Fiber 0 g; Sugar 0.5 g;

Mozzarella Meatball Sandwiches with Basil

Prep T: 5 min | Cook T: 10 min | Servings: 4

Ingredients

- 12 frozen meatballs
- 8 slices Mozzarella cheese
- 4 sub rolls, halved lengthwise
- 64 ml marinara sauce, warmed
- 12 fresh basil leaves

Directions

1. Place the crisper tray on the air fry position. Select Air Fry, set the temperature to 350 F (177 C), and set the time to 10 min.
2. Place the meatballs in the crisper tray. Air fry for 5 min.
3. After 5 min, shake the crisper tray of meatballs. Place the crisper tray back in the grill to resume cooking.
4. While the meatballs are cooking, place two slices of Mozzarella cheese on each sub roll. Use a spoon to spread the marinara sauce on top of the cheese slices. Press three leaves of basil into the sauce on each roll.
5. When cooking is complete, place three meatballs on each sub roll. Serve immediately.

Nutrition: Calories 214; Fat 15.5 g; Carbohydrates 7 g; Protein 6 g; Fiber 2 g; Sugar 3 g;

Air Fryer Rib-Eye Steak

Prep/Cook Time: 2 hrs 25 min | Servings: 2

Ingredients

- 2 rib-eye steaks, cut 2.5 cm thick
- 4 teaspoons grill seasoning (such as Montreal Steak Seasoning)
- 32 ml olive oil
- 1/2 cup reduced-sodium soy sauce

Directions

1. Combine steaks, soy sauce, olive oil, and seasoning in a large resealable bag.
2. Marinate meat for at least 2 hours.
3. Remove steaks from bag and discard the marinade. Pat excess oil off the steaks.
4. Add about 1 tablespoon water to the bottom of the air fryer pan to prevent it from smoking during the cooking process.
5. Preheat the air fryer to 400 F (200 C).
6. Add steaks to air fryer and cook for 7 min. Turn steaks and cook for another 7 min utes until steak is medium rare. For a medium steak, increase the total cook time to 16 min, flipping steak after 8 min utes.
7. Remove steaks, keep warm, and let sit for about 4 min before serving.

Nutrition: Calories 738.5; Fat 65.5 g; Carbohydrates 0 g; Protein 35 g; Fiber 0 g; Sugar 0 g;

Pork Loin Roast with Spice Rub

Prep T: 10 min | Cook T: 45 min | Servings: 4

Ingredients

*   1 (4-pound / 1.8-kg) bone-in pork loin roast

Brine:

*   3 quarts of water
*   64 g of table salt (128 g kosher salt)
*   32 g brown sugar

Spice Rub:

*   4 of cloves garlic, minced or pressed with a garlic press
*   1 tsp minced rosemary
*   1 tsp fresh ground black pepper
*   1⁄2 tsp hot red pepper flakes

Directions

1. Mix brine's ingredients in a very large container and stir until the salt and sugar dissolve. Submerge the pork in the brine. Store in the refrigerator for 4-8 hours.
2. One hour before cooking, remove the pork from the brine and pat dry with paper towels. Mix the ingredients in a tiny bowl, then rub over the pork shoulder, working the rub into any meat's natural seams. Truss the pork roast, skewer it on the rotisserie spit and secure it with the rotisserie forks. Let the pork rest at room temperature.
3. Select Grill, set the temperature to 450 F (235 C) and set the time to 45 min. Set a drip tray in the middle of the grill.
4. Put the spit in the grill and make sure the drip tray is centered beneath the pork roast. Cook the pork until it reaches 135 F (57 C) in its thickest part.

5. Remove now the pork from the rotisserie spit, remove the twine trussing the roast. Pay attention during the process because the spit and forks are hot. Let the pork rest for 15 min, then slice and serve.

Nutrition: Calories 604; Fat 22 g; Carbohydrates 0 g; Protein 95 g ; Fiber 0 g; Sugar 1 g;

Lamb Stew

Prep T: 5 minutes | Cook T: 30 minutes | Servings: 4

Ingredients

*   128 g eggplant, cubed 2 garlic cloves, minced
*   3 celery ribs, chopped
*   64 ml keto tomato sauce
*   454 g lamb stew meat, cubed
*   1 tbsp olive oil
*   Salt and black pepper to the taste

Directions

1. Heat up a pan that fits the air fryer with the oil over medium-high heat, add the lamb, salt, pepper and the garlic and brown for 5 minutes.
2. Add the rest of the ingredients, toss, introduce the pan in the machine and cook at 188 C/370 F for 25 minutes.
3. Divide into bowls and serve for lunch.

Nutrition: Calories: 235; Fat: 14g; Fiber: 3g; Carbs: 5g; Protein:14g

Air Fried Beef Tenderloin

Prep T: 15 min | Cook T: 47 min | Servings: 8

Ingredients

*   908 g beef tenderloin
*   1 tbsp. vegetable oil
*   1 tbsp. dried oregano
*   1 tbsp. salt
*   1/2 tbsp. black pepper, cracked

Directions

1. Pat dries tenderloin with paper towel and places it on a platter.
2. Drizzle vegetable oil and sprinkle oregano, salt, and pepper. Rub the spices on the meat until well coated.

3. Select the air fry setting. Set temperature at 199 C/390 F for 22 min. Reduce now the temperature to 182 C/360 F and cook for 10 min.
4. Set the meat to a plate and allow to rest while tented with paper foil for 10 min before serving.

Nutrition: Calories 235; Fat 10.6 g; Carbohydrates 0.2 g; Sugar 0 g; Protein 32.4 g;

Pork Tenders with Bell Peppers

Prep T: 5 min | Cook T: 15 min | Servings: 4

Ingredients

- 311 g Pork Tenderloin
- 1Bell Pepper, in thin strips
- 1 Red Onion, sliced
- 1Tsps. Provencal Herbs
- Black Pepper to taste
- 1 tbsp. Olive Oil
- 1/2 tbsp. Mustard

Directions

1. Preparing the Ingredients. Preheat the Pro Breeze air fryer to 199 C/390 F.
2. In the oven dish, mix the bell pepper strips with the onion, herbs, and some salt and pepper to taste.
3. Attach half a tbsp of olive oil
4. Divide the pork tenderloin into four pieces and rub it with salt, pepper, and mustard.
5. Thinly coat the pieces with remaining olive oil and place them upright in the oven dish on top of the pepper mixture
6. Air Frying. Place the bowl into the Air fryer. Set the timer to 20 min and roast the meat and the vegetables
7. Turn the meat and mix the peppers halfway through
8. Serve with a fresh salad

Nutrition: Calories: 220Protein: 23.79 g; Fat: 12.36 g; Carbohydrates: 2.45g

Beef and Sauce

Prep T: 5 minutes | Cook T: 20 minutes | Servings: 4

Ingredients

- 454 g lean beef meat, cubed and browned

- 2 garlic cloves, minced
- Salt and black pepper to the taste
- Cooking Spray
- 454 ml keto tomato sauce

Directions

1. Preheat the Air Fryer at 204 C/400 F, add the pan inside, grease it with cooking spray, add the meat and all the other ingredients, toss and cook for 20 minutes.
2. Divide into bowls and serve for lunch.

Nutrition: Calories: 270; Fat: 15g; Fiber: 3g; Carbs: 6g; Protein:12g

Pork Taquitos

Prep T: 10 min | Cook T: 16 min | Servings: 8

Ingredients

- 1juiced lime
- 10 whole-wheat tortillas
- 21/2 C. of shredded mozzarella cheese
- 850 g of cooked, shredded pork tenderloin

Directions

1. Preparing the Ingredients. Ensure your air fryer is preheated to 193 C/380 F.
2. Drizzle now the pork with lime juice and gently mix.
3. Heat tortillas in the microwave with a dampened paper towel to soften.
4. Add about 85 g of pork and 32 g of shredded cheese to each tortilla. Tightly roll them up.
5. Spray the Pro Breeze air fryer basket with a bit of olive oil.
6. Air Frying. Set temperature to 193 C/380 F, and set time to 10 min. Air fry taquitos 7-10 min till tortillas turn a slight golden color, making sure to flip halfway through the cooking process.

Nutrition: Calories: 309; Fat: 11g; Protein: 21g; Sugar: 2g;

Apple-Glazed Pork

Prep T: 15 min | Cook T: 19 min | Servings: 4

Ingredients

- 1 sliced apple
- 1 small onion, sliced
- 2 tbsp apple cider vinegar, divided
- 1/2 tsp thyme
- 1/2 tsp rosemary
- 1/4 tsp brown sugar
- 3 tbsp olive oil, divided
- 1/4 tsp smoked paprika
- 4 pork chops
- Salt and ground black pepper, to taste

Directions

1. Place the baking pan on the bake position. Select Bake, set the temperature to 350 F (177 C), and set the time to 4 min.
2. Combine the apple slices, onion, 1 tbsp of vinegar, thyme, rosemary, brown sugar, and 2 tbsp of olive oil in the baking pan. Stir to mix well.
3. Bake for 4 min.
4. Meanwhile, mix remaining vinegar and olive oil, paprika in a large bowl. Sprinkle with salt and ground black pepper. Stir to mix well. Dredge the pork in the mixture and toss to coat well.
5. Remove the baking pan from the grill and put in the pork. Air fry for 10 min to lightly brown the pork. Flip the pork chops halfway through.
6. Remove the pork from the grill and baste with baked apple mixture on both sides. Put the pork back to the grill and air fry for an additional 5 min. Flip halfway through.
7. Serve immediately.

Nutrition: Calories 531; Fat 33 g; Carbohydrates 5.5 g; Protein 41 g; Fiber 0.5 g; Sugar 4.3 g;

Easy Spicy Steaks with Salad

Prep T: 15 min | Cook T: 15 min | Servings: 4

Ingredients

- 1 (1 1/2-pound / 680-g) boneless top sirloin steak, trimmed and halved crosswise
- 1.1/2 tsps chili powder
- 1.1/2 tsps ground cumin
- 3/4 tsp ground coriander
- 1/8 tsp cayenne pepper
- 1/8 tsp ground cinnamon
- 1.1/4 tsps plus 1/8 tsp salt, divided
- 1/2 tsp plus 1/8 tsp ground black pepper, divided
- 1 tsp plus 1 1/2 tbsp extra-virgin olive oil, divided
- 3 tbsp mayonnaise
- 1.1/2 tbsp white wine vinegar
- 1 tbsp minced fresh dill
- 1 small garlic clove, minced
- 227 g sugar snap peas, strings removed and cut in half on bias
- 1/2 English cucumber, halved lengthwise and sliced thin
- 2 radishes, trimmed, halved and sliced thin
- 256 g baby arugula

Directions

1. In a bowl, coriander, cumin, cayenne pepper, mix chili powder, cinnamon, 1.1/4 tsps salt and 1/2 tsp pepper until well combined.
2. Add the steaks to another bowl and pat dry with paper towels. Brush with 1 tsp oil and

56

transfer to the bowl of spice mixture. Roll over to coat thoroughly.

3. Arrange the coated steaks in the air fry basket, spaced evenly apart.
4. Place the basket on the air fry position.
5. Select Air Fry. Set temperature to 400 F (205 C) and set time to 15 min. Flip the steak halfway through to ensure even cooking.
6. When cooking is done, an instant-read thermometer inserted into the thickest part of the meat should register at least 145 degs F (63 degs C).

7. Transfer the steaks to a clean work surface and wrap with aluminum foil. Let stand while preparing salad.
8. To make the salad stir together in a large bowl 1.1⁄2 tbsp of olive oil, vinegar, mayonnaise, dill, garlic, 1⁄8 tsp pepper, and 1⁄8 tsp salt. Add snap peas, cucumber, radishes and arugula. Toss to blend well.
9. Slice now the steaks and serve with the salad.

Nutrition: Calories 380; Fat 19 g; Carbohydrates 4 g; Protein 45 g; Fiber 1.2 g; Sugar 2 g;

Garlicky Shrimp Caesar Salad

Prep T: 10 min | Cook T: 5 min | Servings: 4

Ingredients

- 1 pound (454 g) fresh jumbo shrimp
- Juice of 1/2 lemon
- 3 garlic cloves, minced
- Sea salt, to taste
- Freshly ground black pepper, to taste
- 2 heads romaine lettuce, chopped
- 96 g Caesar dressing
- 64 g grated Parmesan cheese

Directions

1. Place the grill plate on the grill position. Select Grill, set the temperature to 450 F (232 C), and set the time to 5 min.
2. Get a bowl and mix the shrimp with lemon juice, garlic, salt, and pepper in it. Let marinate for 10 min.
3. Place the shrimp on the grill plate. Grill for 5 min.
4. While the shrimp grills, toss romaine lettuce with Caesar dressing, divide evenly among four plates or bowls.
5. When cooking is done, use tongs to remove the shrimp from the grill and place on top of each salad. Sprinkle with the Parmesan cheese and serve.

Nutrition: Calories 102; Fat 4.5 g; Carbohydrates 11.5 g; Protein 3.3 g; Fiber 1 g; Sugar 1.2 g;

Garlic Butter Lobster Tails

Prep T: 15 min | Cook T: 8 min | Servings: 2

Ingredients

- 2 lobster tails
- 2 cloves garlic, minced
- 2 tbsp butter
- 1 tsp lemon juice
- 1 tsp chopped chives
- Salt to taste

Directions

1. Butterfly the lobster tails.
2. Place now the meat on top of the shell.
3. Mix the remaining ingredients in a bowl.
4. Add lobster tails inside the air fryer.
5. Set it to air fry.
6. Spread garlic butter on the meat.
7. Cook at 193 C/380 F for 5 min.
8. Spread more butter on top.
9. Cook for another 2 to 3 min.

Serving Suggestions: Garnish with chopped chives.

Prep & Cooking Tips: You can use frozen lobster tails for this recipe but extend cooking time to 12 min.

Nutrition: Calories 217; Fat 12.5 g; Carbohydrates 0 g; Protein 24.5 g; Fiber 0 g; Sugar 0 g;

Parmesan Salmon Fillets

Prep T: 5 minutes | Cook T: 15 minutes | Servings: 4

Ingredients

- 4 salmon fillets, skinless

- 1 tsp mustard
- A pinch of salt and black pepper
- 64 g coconut flakes
- 1 tbsp parmesan, grated
- Cooking Spray

Directions

1. Get a bowl and mix in the parmesan with the other ingredients except the fish and cooking spray and stir well.
2. Coat the fish in this mix, grease it with cooking spray and arrange in the air fryer's basket.
3. Cook at 204 C/400 F for 15 minutes, divide between plates and serve with a side salad.

Nutrition: Calories: 240; Fat: 13g; Fiber: 3g; Carbs: 6g; Protein:15g

Halibut Steaks

Prep T: 15 minutes | Cook T: 10 minutes | Servings: 4

Ingredients

- 680 g halibut steaks (170 g each fillet)
- ½ tsp salt
- ½ tsp ground black pepper
- 114 g bacon, sliced
- 1 tbsp sunflower oil

Directions

1. Cut every halibut fillet on 2 parts and sprinkle with salt and ground black pepper. Then wrap the fish fillets in the sliced bacon.
2. Preheat the air fryer to 204 C/400 F. Sprinkle the halibut bites with sunflower oil and put in the air fryer basket.
3. Cook the meal for 5 minutes. Then flip the fish bites on another side and cook them for 5 minutes more.

Nutrition: Calories: 375; Fat: 19.4g; Fiber: 0.1g; Carbs: 0.6g; Protein:46.5g

Ranch Tilapia

Prep T: 15 min | Cook T: 13 min | Servings: 4

Ingredients

- 96 g cornflakes, crushed
- 1 (28 g) packet dry ranch-style dressing mix
- 134 ml vegetable oil

- 2 eggs
- 4 (170 g) tilapia fillets

Directions

1. In a shallow bowl, beat the eggs.
2. In another bowl, add the cornflakes, ranch dressing, and oil and mix until a crumbly mixture form.
3. Dip the fish fillets into egg and then, coat with the breadcrumb's mixture.
4. Choose "Power Button" of Air Fry Oven and select the "Air Fry" mode.
5. Choose the Time button and set the cooking time to 13 min.
6. Now press the Temp button and set the temperature at 180 C/356 F.
7. Press "Start/Pause" button to start.
8. After the Air Fryer is preheated, open the lid.
9. Arrange the tilapia fillets in greased "Air Fry Basket" and insert in the oven.
10. Serve hot.

Nutrition: Calories 267; Fat 12.2g; Protein 34.9g; Carbs: 2.6g;

Teriyaki Salmon with Bok Choy

Prep T: 15 min | Cook T: 15 min | Servings: 4

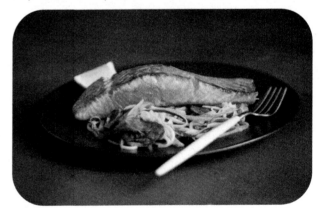

Ingredients

- 96 g Teriyaki sauce , divided
- 4 (170-g) skinless salmon fillets
- 4 heads baby bok choy, ends trimmed off and cut in half lengthwise through the root
- 1 tsp sesame oil
- 1 tbsp vegetable oil
- 1 tbsp toasted sesame seeds

Directions

1. Set aside 32 g of Teriyaki sauce and pour the remaining sauce into a resealable plastic

bag. Put the salmon into the bag and seal, squeezing as much air out as possible. Allow the salmon to marinate for at least 10 min.

2. Arrange the bok choy halves on the sheet pan. Drizzle the oils over the vegetables, tossing to coat. Drizzle about 1 tbsp of the reserved Teriyaki sauce over the bok choy, then push them to the sides of the sheet pan.
3. Put now salmon fillets in the middle of the sheet pan.
4. Place the pan on the toast position.
5. Select Toast, set temperature to 375 degs F (190 degs C), and set time to 15 min.
6. When done, remove the pan and brush the salmon with the remaining Teriyaki sauce. Serve garnished with sesame seeds.

Nutrition: Calories 253; Fat 11 g; Carbohydrates 2 g; Protein 34 g; Fiber 2.5 g; Sugar 2 g;

Basil Scallops

Prep T: 15 minutes | Cook T: 6 minutes | Servings: 4

Ingredients

- 340 g scallops
- 1 tbsp dried basil
- ½ tsp salt
- 1 tbsp coconut oil, melted

Directions

1. Mix up salt, coconut oil, and dried basil. Brush the scallops with basil mixture and leave for 5 minutes to marinate. Meanwhile, preheat the air fryer to 204 C/400 F.
2. Put the marinated scallops in the air fryer and sprinkle them with remaining coconut oil and basil mixture.
3. Cook the scallops for 4 minutes. Then flip them on another side and cook for 2 minutes more.

Nutrition: Calories: 104; Fat: 4.1g; Fiber: 0g; Carbs: 2g; Protein:14.3g

Cheesy Crab Toasts

Prep T: 10 min | Cook T: 5 min | Makes 15 to 18

toasts

Ingredients

- 1 (170-g) can flaked crab meat, well drained
- 3 tbsp light mayonnaise
- 32 g shredded Parmesan cheese
- 32 g shredded Cheddar cheese
- 1 tsp Worcestershire sauce
- ½ tsp lemon juice
- 1 loaf artisan bread, French bread, or baguette, cut into 1 cm-thick slices

Directions

1. Place the crisper tray on the bake position. Select Bake, set the temperature to 360 F (182 C), and set the time to 5 min.
2. In a large bowl, stir together all your ingredients except the bread slices.
3. On a clean work surface, lay the bread slices. Spread 1⁄2 tbsp of crab mixture onto each slice of bread.
4. Arrange the bread slices in the crisper tray in a single layer. You'll need to work in batches to avoid overcrowding.
5. Bake for 5 min until the tops are lightly browned.
6. Transfer to a plate and repeat with the remaining bread slices.
7. Serve warm.

Nutrition: Calories 51; Fat 2.3 g; Carbohydrates 4 g; Protein 3.4 g; Fiber 0.1 g; Sugar 0.3 g;

Tilapia Tacos

Prep T: 10 min | Cook T: 10 to 15 min | Servings: 6

Ingredients

- 1 tbsp avocado oil
- 1 tbsp Cajun seasoning
- 4 (142 to 170 g) tilapia fillets
- 1 (397-g) package coleslaw mix
- 12 corn tortillas
- 2 limes, cut into wedges

Directions

1. Line a baking pan with parchment paper.
2. In a shallow bowl, stir together the avocado oil and Cajun seasoning to make a marinade. Place the tilapia fillets into the bowl, turning to coat evenly.
3. Put the fillets in the baking pan in a single layer.
4. Slide the pan into the air fryer grill.
5. Select Air Fry, set temperature to 375 degs F (190 degs C), and set time to 10 min.
6. When cooked, the fish should be flaky. If necessary, continue cooking for 5 min more. Remove the fish from the air fryer grill to a plate.
7. Assemble the tacos: Spoon some of the coleslaw mix into each tortilla and top each with 1/3 of a tilapia fillet. Squeeze lime juice over the top of each taco and serve immediately.

Nutrition: Calories 520; Fat 18 g; Carbohydrates 57 g; Protein 31 g; Fiber 4.5 g; Sugar 11.5 g;

Salmon and Creamy Chives Sauce

Prep T: 5 minutes | Cook T: 20 minutes | Servings: 4

Ingredients

- 4 salmon fillets, boneless
- A pinch of salt and black pepper
- 64 g heavy cream
- 1 tbsp chives, chopped
- 1 tsp lemon juice
- 1 tsp dill, chopped
- 2 garlic cloves, minced
- 32 g ghee, melted

Directions

1. Get a bowl and combine all the ingredients in it (leave the salmon aside). Arrange the salmon in a pan that fits the air fryer, drizzle the sauce all over, introduce the pan in the machine and cook at 182 C/360 F for 20 minutes.
2. Divide everything between plates and serve.

Nutrition: Calories: 220; Fat: 14g; Fiber: 2g; Carbs: 5g; Protein:12g

Easy Shrimp and Vegetable Paella

Prep T: 5 min | Cook T: 14 to 17 min | Servings: 4

Ingredients

- 1 (284-g) package frozen cooked rice, thawed
- 1 (170-g) jar artichoke hearts, drained and chopped
- 32 ml vegetable broth
- 1/2 tsp dried thyme
- 1/2 tsp turmeric
- 128 g frozen cooked small shrimp
- 64 g frozen baby peas
- 1 tomato, diced

Directions

1. Place the baking pan on the bake position. Select Bake, set the temperature to 340 F (171 C), and set the time to 17 min.
2. Combine together cooked rice, chopped artichoke hearts, vegetable broth, thyme, and turmeric in the baking pan and stir to combine.
3. Bake for 9 min, or until the rice is heated through.
4. Remove the pan from the grill and fold in the shrimp, baby peas, and diced tomato and mix well.
5. Return to the grill and continue baking for 5 to 8 min, or until the shrimp are done and the paella is bubbling. Cool for 5 min before serving.

Nutrition: Calories 320; Fat 3 g; Carbohydrates 64 g; Protein 7 g; Fiber 3 g; Sugar 0.3 g;

Tuna Steaks with Red Onions

Prep T: 10 min| Cook T: 10 min| Servings: 4

Ingredients

- 4 tuna steaks
- 1/2 pound (227 g) red onions
- 1 tsp dried rosemary
- 1 tbsp cayenne pepper
- 1 lemon, sliced

Directions

1. Warm the air fryer to 400 F (205 C) and spray the basket with cooking spray.
2. Place the tuna steaks in the basket and scatter the onions all over. Sprinkle with the olive oil and sprinkle with rosemary, cayenne pepper, salt, and black pepper.
3. Bake in batches in the preheated air fryer for 10 min until cooked through.
4. Garnish with the lemon slices and serve warm.

Nutrition: Calories: 488; Fat: 19.2g; Carbs: 7.1g; Protein: 68.1g;

Salmon Burgers

Prep T: 20 min | Cook T: 22 min | Servings: 6

Ingredients

- 3 large russet potatoes, peeled and cubed
- 1 (170 g) cooked salmon fillet
- 1 egg
- 96 g frozen vegetables (of your choice), parboiled and drained
- 2 tbsp fresh parsley, chopped
- 1 tsp fresh dill, chopped
- Salt and ground black pepper, as required
- 128 g breadcrumbs
- 32 ml olive oil

Directions

1. In a pan of the boiling water, cook the potatoes for about 10 min.
2. Drain the potatoes well.
3. Set the potatoes into a bowl and mash with a potato masher.
4. Set aside to cool completely.

5. In another bowl, add the salmon and flake with a fork.
6. Add the cooked potatoes, egg, parboiled vegetables, parsley, dill, salt and black pepper and mix until well combined.
7. Make 6 equal-sized patties from the mixture.
8. Coat patties with breadcrumb evenly and then drizzle with the oil evenly.
9. Choose "Power Button" of Air Fry Oven and select the "Air Fry" mode.
10. Choose the Time button and set the cooking time to 12 min.
11. Now press the Temp button and set the temperature at 355 degs F.
12. Press "Start/Pause" button to start.
13. After the Air Fryer is preheated, open the lid.
14. Arrange the patties in the greased air fryer's basket and insert in the oven.
15. Flip the patties once halfway through.
16. Serve hot.

Nutrition: Calories 334; Fat 12.1g; Protein 12.5g; Carbs: 1.5 g;

Beer Battered Fish

Prep T: 10 min | Cook T: 12 min | Servings: 5
Ingredients

- 128 g of all-purpose flour
- 2 tbsp. of cornstarch
- 1/2 tsp. of baking soda
- 170 g of beer
- 1 egg beaten
- 96 g of all-purpose flour
- 1/2 tsp. of paprika
- 1 tsp. of salt
- 1/4 tsp. of ground black pepper
- Pinch of cayenne pepper
- 2.5 K of cod cut into 4 or 5 pieces
- Vegetable oil

Directions

1. Merge the 128 g of flour, cornstarch and baking soda in a large bowl and add the beer and egg, stir until it's smooth. Seal the bowl of batter with plastic wrap and refrigerate for at least 20 min.
2. Combine the 96 g of flour, paprika, salt, black pepper and cayenne pepper in a shallow dredging pan.

3. Set the cod fish fillets dry with a paper towel. Now dip the fish into the batter, coating all sides and allow the excess batter to drip off, then coat each fillet with seasoned flour.
4. Whisk any leftover flour on the fish fillets and pat gently to adhere the flour to the batter. After that, pre-heat your air fryer at 199 C/390 F.
5. Air-fry for 12 min at 199 C/390 F. Serve with lemon wedges, malt vinegar and tartar sauce.

Nutrition: Calories: 265; Fat: 16g;Carbohydrates: 1g; Fiber: 0g; Protein: 39g;

Sumptuous Seafood Casserole

Prep T: 8 min | Cook T: 22 min | Servings: 2

Ingredients

- 1 tbsp olive oil
- 1 small yellow onion, chopped
- 2 garlic cloves, minced
- 113 g tilapia pieces
- 113 g rockfish pieces
- 1/2 tsp dried basil
- Salt and ground white pepper, to taste
- 4 eggs, lightly beaten
- 1 tbsp dry sherry
- 4 tbsp cheese, shredded

Directions

1. Warm up the olive oil in a nonstick skillet over medium-high heat until shimmering.
2. Add now garlic, onion and sauté for 2 min or until fragrant.
3. Add the rockfish, tilapia, salt, basil, and white pepper to the skillet. Sauté to combine well and transfer them on a baking pan.

4. Combine the eggs, cheese and sherry in a large bowl. Stir to mix well. Pour the mixture in the baking pan over the fish mixture.
5. Place the pan on the bake position.
6. Select Bake, set temperature to 360 F (182 C) and set time to 20 min.
7. When cooking is done, the eggs should be set and the casserole edges should be lightly browned. Serve immediately.

Nutrition: Calories 415; Fat 24 g; Carbohydrates 8 g; Protein 36 g; Fiber 1 g; Sugar 3 g;

Paprika Shrimp

Prep T: 5 min | Cook T: 10 min | Servings: 4

Ingredients

- 1 pound (454 g) tiger shrimp
- 2 tbsp olive oil
- 1/2 tbsp old bay seasoning
- 1/4 tbsp smoked paprika
- 1/4 tsp cayenne pepper
- A pinch of sea salt

Directions

1. Place the crisper tray on the air fry position. Select Air Fry, set the temperature to 380 F (193 C), and set the time to 10 min.
2. Get a bowl, combine all the ingredients in it in order to season the shrimps well.
3. Arrange the shrimp in the crisper tray. Air fry for 10 min, shaking the crisper tray halfway through, or until the shrimp are pink and cooked through.
4. Serve hot.

Nutrition: Calories 100; Fat 0.5 g; Carbohydrates 0 g; Protein 22.5 g; Fiber 0 g; Sugar 0 g;

Fast Bacon-Wrapped Scallops

Prep T: 5 min | Cook T: 10 min | Servings: 4

Ingredients

- 8 slices bacon, cut in half
- 16 sea scallops, patted dry
- Cooking Spray
- Salt, freshly ground black pepper, to taste
- 16 toothpicks, soaked for at least 30 min

Directions

1. On a clean work surface, wrap half of a slice of bacon around each scallop and secure with a toothpick.
2. Lay the bacon-wrapped scallops in the air fry basket in a single layer.
3. Spritz the scallops with cooking spray and sprinkle the salt and pepper to season.
4. Place the basket on the air fry position.
5. Select Air Fry, set temperature to 370 F (188 C), and set time to 10 min. Flip now scallops halfway through the cooking time.
6. When cooking is done, bacon should be cooked through and the scallops should be firm. Remove the scallops from the air fryer grill to a plate Serve warm.

Nutrition: Calories 125.5; Fat 8 g; Carbohydrates 4 g; Protein 9 g; Fiber 1 g; Sugar 3 g;

Cajun shrimp

Prep T: 5 min | Cook T: 10 min | Servings: 4-6

Ingredients

1. Olive oil (1 tbsp)
2. Old Bay seasoning (0.5 tsp.)
3. Tiger shrimp (567 g or 16-20 shrimps)
4. Smoked paprika (0.25 tsp.)
5. Cayenne pepper (0.25 tsp.)
6. Salt (1 pinch)

Directions

- Heat the air fryer to 390 Fahrenheit / 199 Celsius.
- Combine each of the fasteners and coat the shrimp with the oil and spices.
- Put the shrimp in the basket and fry for five min.
- Enjoy shrimp with a portion of rice.

Nutrition: Calories: 147; Total Fat: 5g; Carbohydrates: 10g; Fiber: 4g; Protein: 16g;

Cod Steaks with Ginger

Prep T: 15 min | Cook T: 30 min | Servings: 2

Ingredients

1. Large cod steaks (2 slices)
2. Turmeric powder (0.25 tsp.)
3. Salt and pepper (1 pinch)
4. Powdered ginger (0.5 tsp.)
5. Garlic powder (0.5 tsp.)
6. Plum sauce (1 tbsp)
7. Slices of ginger (to taste)
8. Flour topped with Kentucky kernels (+) cornmeal (1 part of each)

Directions

1. Dry the cod steaks with several paper towels. Put the cod in a marinade for a few min (based on pepper, salt, ginger powder and turmeric powder).
2. Lightly coat each of the steaks with the cornmeal and Kentucky mixture.
3. Set the temperature in the air fryer to 356 F / 180 C.
4. Airs fry them for 15 min. Increase the temperature setting to 400 Fahrenheit / 204 Celsius for five min.
5. Prepare the sauce in a wok. Brown the ginger slices and places the pan on a cold stove. Stir in the plum sauce. Dilute the sauce (just enough) with a little water.
6. Serve the steaks with a drizzle of sauce.

Nutrition: Calories: 180; Fat: 13g; Protein: 5g; Carbs: 14g; Net Carbs: 10g; Fiber: 4g;

Green Curry Shrimp

Prep T: 15 min | Cook T: 5 min | Servings: 4

Ingredients

- 1 to 2 tbsp of Thai green curry paste
- 2 tbsp coconut oil, melted

- 1 tbsp half-and-half or coconut milk
- 1 tsp fish sauce
- 1 tsp soy sauce
- 1 tsp minced fresh ginger
- 1 clove garlic, minced
- 1 pound (454 g) jumbo raw shrimp, peeled and deveined
- 32 g chopped fresh Thai basil or sweet basil
- 32 g chopped fresh cilantro

Directions

1. In the baking pan, combine the curry paste, coconut oil, half-and-half, fish sauce, soy sauce, ginger, and garlic. Whisk until well combined.
2. Add now shrimp, toss until well coated. Now marinate at room temperature for 15 to 30 min.
3. Place the crisper tray on the air fry position. Select Air Fry, set the temperature to 400 F (204 C), and set the time to 5 min.
4. Air fry for 5 min, stirring halfway through cooking time.
5. Transfer now shrimp to a serving bowl or platter. Garnish with the basil and cilantro. Serve immediately.

Nutrition: Calories 156; Fat 7 g; Carbohydrates 0 g; Protein 22.5 g; Fiber 0 g; Sugar 0 g;

Buttered Salmon

Prep T: 10 min | Cook T: 10 min | Servings: 2

Ingredients

- 2 (170 g) salmon fillets

- Salt and ground black pepper, as required
- 1 tbsp butter, melted

Directions

1. Flavor each salmon fillet with salt and black pepper and then, coat with the butter.
2. Choose "Power Button" of Air Fry Oven and select the "Air Fry" mode.
3. Choose the Time button and set the cooking time to 10 min.
4. Now press the Temp button and set the temperature at 182 C/360 F.
5. Press "Start/Pause" button to start.
6. After the Air Fryer is preheated, open the lid.
7. Arrange the salmon fillets in greased "Air Fry Basket" and insert in the oven.
8. Serve hot.

Nutrition: Calories 276; Fat 16.3g; Protein 33.1g; Carbs: 2.1;

Chili Tuna Cakes

Prep T: 33 min | Cook T: 25 min | Servings: 4

Ingredients

- 142 g of canned tuna
- 1 tsp. lime juice
- 1 tsp. paprika
- 32 g flour
- 64 ml milk
- 1 small onion, diced
- 2 eggs
- 1 tsp. chili powder, optional
- 1/2 tsp. salt

Directions

1. Merge all ingredients in a bowl and mix well to combine.
2. Make two large patties, or a few smaller ones, out of the mixture.
3. Place them on a lined sheet and refrigerate for 30 min.
4. Cook the patties for 7 min on each side at 177 C/350 F.

Nutrition: Calories 125; Fat 1.9 g; Carbohydrates 11.2 g; Sugar 0 g; Protein 15.2 g;

Lemony Raspberry Muffins

Prep T: 5 min | Cook T: 15 min | Servings: 6

Ingredients

- 256 g almond flour
- 96 g Swerve
- 1.1⁄4 tsps baking powder
- 1⁄3 tsp ground allspice
- 1⁄3 tsp ground anise star
- 1⁄2 tsp grated lemon zest
- 1⁄4 tsp salt
- 2 eggs
- 128 g sour cream
- 64 ml coconut oil
- 64 g raspberries

Directions

1. Line now a muffin pan with 6 paper liners.
2. In a mixing bowl, mix the almond flour, baking powder, Swerve, lemon zest, allspice, anise, and salt.
3. In another bowl, beat the eggs, coconut oil, and sour cream until well mixed. Add the egg mixture to the flour mixture and stir to combine. Mix in the raspberries.
4. Scrape now the batter into the prepared muffin cups, filling each about three-quarters full.
5. Place the muffin pan on the bake position.
6. Select Bake, set temperature to 345 F (174 C), and set time to 15 min.
7. When cooking is complete, the tops should be golden and a toothpick inserted in the middle should come out clean.

8. Allow muffins to cool down for 10 min in the muffin pan before removing and serving.

Fried Bananas with Chocolate Sauce

Prep T: 10 min | Cook T: 10 min |Serving: 2

Ingredients

- 1 large egg
- 32 g cornstarch
- 32 g plain bread crumbs
- 3 bananas halved crosswise
- Cooking oil
- Chocolate sauce

Directions

1. In a small bowl, beat the egg. In another bowl, place the cornstarch.
2. Place the breadcrumbs in a third bowl.
3. Dip the bananas in the cornstarch, then the egg, and then the breadcrumbs.
4. Spray the air fryer basket with cooking oil. Place the bananas in the basket and spray them with cooking oil.
5. Set temperature to 182 C/360 F and cook for 5 min. Open the air fryer and flip the bananas—Cook for an additional 2 min. Transfer the bananas to plates.
6. Drizzle the chocolate sauce over the bananas and serve.
7. You can make your chocolate sauce using two tbsp of milk and 32 g of chocolate chips. Heat a saucepan over medium-high heat. Add the milk and stir for 1 to 2 min. Add the chocolate chips. Stir for 2 min, or until the chocolate has melted.

Nutrition: Calories: 20; Fat: 6g; Protein: 3g; Fiber: 3g;

Caramelized Peaches

Prep T: 10 min | Cook T: 10 min | Servings: 6

Ingredients

- 3 peaches, peeled, halved, and pitted
- 2 tbsp packed brown sugar
- 128 g plain Greek yogurt
- 1/4 tsp ground cinnamon
- 1 tsp pure vanilla extract
- 128 g fresh blueberries

Directions

1. Arrange the peaches in the air fry basket, cut-side up. Top with a very generous sprinkle of brown sugar.
2. Place the basket on the bake position.
3. Select Bake, set temperature to 380 F (193 C), and set time to 10 min.
4. Meanwhile, whisk together the cinnamon, vanilla, and yogurt in a small bowl until smooth.
5. When cooking is done, peaches should be lightly browned, caramelized.
6. Remove the peaches from the air fryer grill to a plate. Now serve topped with yogurt mixture and fresh blueberries.

Nutrition: Calories 40; Fat 0 g; Carbohydrates 7.5 g; Protein 13 g; Fiber 0.8 g; Sugar 7 g;

Chocolate-Coconut Cake

Prep T: 5 min | Cook T: 15 min | Servings: 10

Ingredients

- 160 g unsweetened bakers' chocolate
- 1 stick butter
- 1 tsp liquid stevia
- 42.5 g shredded coconut
- 2 tbsp coconut milk
- 2 eggs, beaten
- Cooking Spray

Directions

1. Lightly spritz a baking pan with cooking spray.
2. Place the butter, chocolate, and stevia in a microwave-safe bowl. Microwave for about 30 seconds until melted. Let now the chocolate mixture to cool down to room temperature.
3. Add the remaining ingredients to the chocolate mixture and stir until well incorporated. Pour now the batter in the prepared pan.
4. Place the pan on the bake position.
5. Select Bake, set temperature to 330 F (166 C), and set time to 15 min.
6. When cooking is complete, a toothpick inserted in the center should come out clean.
7. Remove from the air fryer grill and allow to cool for about 10 min before serving.

Nutrition: Calories 111.5; Fat 11 g; Carbohydrates 1.8 g; Protein 1.3 g; Fiber 0.1 g; Sugar 1.7 g;

Sponge Cake

Prep T: 15 min | Cook T: 20 min | Servings: 12

Ingredients

- 384 g flour
- 3 tsps baking powder
- 64 g cornstarch
- 1 tsp baking soda
- 128 ml olive oil
- 2 tsps vanilla extract
- 704 ml milk
- 416 g sugar
- 256 ml water
- 32 ml lemon juice

Directions

1. In a bowl, blend flour in with cornstarch, baking powder, baking soda, sugar and whisk well.
2. In another bowl, mix oil in with milk, water, vanilla, lemon juice and whisk.
3. Consolidate the two blends, mix, pour in a lubed baking dish that fits your air fryer, place in the fryer and cook at 177 C/350 F for 20 min.
4. Leave cake to chill off, cut and serve.

Nutrition: Calories 246; Fat 3 g; Carbohydrates 6 g; Sugar 3 g; Protein 2 g; Cholesterol 0 mg;

Butter Crumble

Prep T: 20 minutes | Cook T: 25 minutes | Servings: 4

Ingredients

- 64 g coconut flour
- 2 tbsp butter, softened
- 2 tbsp Erythritol
- 85 g peanuts, crushed
- 1 tbsp cream cheese
- 1 tsp baking powder
- ½ tsp lemon juice

Directions

1. In the mixing bowl mix up coconut flour, butter, Erythritol, baking powder, and lemon juice. Stir the mixture until homogenous. Then place it in the freezer for 10 minutes. Meanwhile, mix up peanuts and cream cheese.

2. Grate the frozen dough. Line the air fryer mold with baking paper. Then put ½ of grated dough in the mold and flatten it.
3. Top it with cream cheese mixture. Then put remaining grated dough over the cream cheese mixture.
4. Place the mold with the crumble in the air fryer and cook it for 25 minutes at 330F.

Nutrition: Calories: 252; Fat: 19.6g; Fiber: 7.8g; Carbs: 13.1g; Protein:8.8g

Chocolate and Peanut Butter Lava Cupcakes

Prep T: 10 min | Cook T: 10 to 13 min | Servings: 8

Ingredients

- Nonstick baking spray with flour
- 170 g chocolate cake mix
- 1 egg
- 1 egg yolk
- 32 g safflower oil
- 32 g hot water
- 42.5 g sour cream
- 3 tbsp peanut butter
- 1 tbsp powdered sugar

Directions

1. Place the baking pan on the bake position. Select Bake, set the temperature to 350 F (177 C), and set the time to 13 min.
2. Double up 16 foil muffin cups to make 8 cups. Spray each lightly with nonstick spray; set aside.
3. In a bowl, mix the water, cake mix, egg, egg yolk, safflower oil, and sour cream, and beat until combined.

4. In a tiny bowl, mix the peanut butter and powdered sugar and mix well. Form this mixture into 8 balls.
5. Spoon about 32 g of the chocolate batter into each muffin cup and top with a peanut butter ball. Spoon remaining batter on top of the peanut butter balls to cover them.
6. Arrange the cups in the pan, leaving some space between each. Bake for 10-13 min or until the tops look dry and set.
7. Let the cupcakes cool for about 10 min, then serve warm.

Berry Cookies

Prep T: 15 minutes | Cook T: 9 minutes | Servings: 4

Ingredients

- 2 tsps butter, softened
- 1 tbsp Splenda
- 1 egg yolk
- 64 g almond flour
- 28 g strawberry, chopped, mashed

Directions

1. In the mixing bowl mix up butter, Splenda, egg yolk, and almond flour. Knead the non-sticky dough. Then make the small balls from the dough. Use your finger to make small holes in every ball. Then fill the balls with mashed strawberries.
2. Preheat the air fryer to 182 C/360 F. Line the air fryer basket with baking paper and put the cookies inside.
3. Cook them for 9 minutes.

Nutrition: Calories: 68; Fat: 4.8g; Fiber: 0.5g; Carbs: 4.4g; Protein:1.5g

Raspberry Pop-Tarts

Prep T: 25 minutes | Cook T: 10 minutes | Servings: 5

Ingredients

- 57 g raspberries
- 64 g almond flour
- 1 egg, beaten
- 1 tbsp butter, softened
- 1 tbsp Erythritol
- ½ tsp baking powder

- 1 egg white, whisked
- Cooking Spray

Directions

1. In the mixing bowl mix up almond flour, egg, butter, and baking powder Knead the soft non-sticky dough. Then mash the raspberries and mix them up with Erythritol. Cut the dough into halves. Then roll up every dough half into the big squares. After this, cut every square into 5 small squares.
2. Put the mashed raspberry mixture on 5 mini squares. Then cover them with remaining dough squares. Secure the edges with the help of the fork. Then brush the pop-tarts with whisked egg white. Preheat the air fryer to 177 C/350 F. Grease now basket of the air fryer with cooking spray.
3. Place the pop tarts in the air fryer basket in one layer. Cook them at 177 C/350 F for 10 minutes. Cool the cooked pop-tarts totally and transfer in the serving plates.

Nutrition: Calories: 59; Fat: 4.7g; Fiber: 1.1g; Carbs: 2.3g; Protein:2.6g

Strawberry Cups

Prep T: 5 minutes | Cook T: 10 minutes | Servings: 8

Ingredients

- 16 strawberries, halved
- 2 tbsp coconut oil
- 256 g chocolate chips, melted

Directions

1. In a pan suitable for your air fryer, mix the strawberries with the oil and the melted chocolate chips, toss gently, put the pan in the air fryer and cook at 171 C/340 F for 10 minutes.
2. Divide into cups and serve cold.

Nutrition: Calories: 162; Fat: 5g; Fiber: 3g; Carbs: 5g; Protein:6g

Pound Cake with Mixed Berries

Prep T: 10 min | Cook T: 8 min | Servings: 6

Ingredients

- 3 tbsp unsalted butter, at room temperature
- 6 slices pound cake, sliced about 2.5 cm thick
- 128 g fresh raspberries
- 128 g fresh blueberries
- 3 tbsp sugar
- 1/2 tbsp fresh mint, minced

Directions

1. Place the grill plate on the grill position. Select Grill, set the temperature to 450 F (232 C), and set the time to 8 min.
2. Evenly spread the butter on both of the sides of each slice of pound cake.
3. Place the pound cake on the grill plate. Grill for 2 min.
4. After 2 min, flip the pound cake and grill for 2 min more, until golden brown. Repeat steps 3-4 for each of the pound cake slices.
5. While the pound cake grills, in a medium mixing bowl, combine the raspberries, blueberries, sugar, and min t.
6. When cooking is complete, plate the cake slices and serve topped with the berry mixture.

Nutrition: Calories 224; Fat 12.5 g; Carbohydrates 26 g; Protein 2.3 g; Fiber 0.7 g; Sugar 16 g;

Fluffy Blueberry Fritters

Prep T: 5min | Cook T: 15 min |Serving: 4

Ingredients

- 96 g all-purpose flour
- 1tsp baking powder
- 64 ml coconut milk
- 2tbsp coconut sugar
- A pinch of sea salt
- 1 egg
- 2tbsp melted butter
- 56 g fresh blueberries

Directions

1. In a mixing bowl, thoroughly mix all the ingredients.
2. Drop a spoonful of batter onto the greased Air Fryer pan. Cook in the preheated Air Fryer at 182 C/360 F for 10 min, flipping them halfway through the cooking time.
3. Repeat now with remaining batter and serve warm. Enjoy!

Nutrition: Calories: 195; Fat 8g; Carbs 25.4g; Protein 4.9 g; Sugars 6.9g; Fiber 1g;

Oaty Chocolate Cookies

Prep T: 10 min | Cook T: 20 min | Makes 4 dozen (1-by-14 cm) bars

Ingredients

- 128 g unsalted butter, at room temperature
- 128 g dark brown sugar
- 64 g granulated sugar
- 2 large eggs
- 1 tbsp vanilla extract
- Pinch salt
- 256 g old-fashioned rolled oats
- 192 g all-purpose flour
- 1 tsp baking powder
- 1 tsp baking soda
- 256 g chocolate chips

Directions

1. Stir together the butter, granulated sugar, and brown sugar in a large mixing bowl until smooth and light in color.

2. Crack the eggs in the bowl, one at a time, mixing after each addition. Stir in the vanilla and salt.
3. Mix together the oats, flour, baking soda, and baking powder in a separate bowl. Add the mixture to the butter mixture and stir until mixed. Stir in the chocolate chips.
4. Spread the dough onto the sheet pan in an even layer.
5. Place the basket on the bake position.
6. Select Bake, set temperature to 350 F (180 C), and set time to 20 min.
7. After 15 min, check the cookie, rotating the pan if the crust is not browning evenly. Continue cooking for a total of 18 to 20 min or until golden brown.
8. When cooking is complete, remove the pan from the air fryer grill and allow to cool completely before slicing and serving.

Nutrition: Calories 377; Fat 26 g; Carbohydrates 21 g; Protein 13 g; Fiber 3 g; Sugar 1 g;

Orange Cinnamon Cookies

Prep T: 15 min | Cook T: 24 min | Servings: 10
Ingredients

- 3 tbsp cream cheese
- 3 tbsp Erythritol
- 1 tsp vanilla extract
- 1/2 tsp ground cinnamon
- 1 egg, beaten
- 128 g almond flour
- 1/2 tsp baking powder
- 1 tsp butter, softened
- 1/2 tsp orange zest, grated

Directions

1. Put the cream cheese and Erythritol in the bowl. Add vanilla extract, ground cinnamon, and almond flour.
2. Stir the mixture with the help of the spoon until homogenous. Then add egg, almond flour, baking powder, and butter. Add orange zest and stir the mass until homogenous. Then knead it with the help of the fingertips.
3. Roll up the dough with the help of the rolling pin. Then make the cookies with the help of the cookies cutter. Preheat the air fryer to 185 C/365 F.

4. Line air fryer basket with baking paper. Put the cookies on the baking paper and cook them for 8 min. The time of cooking depends on the cooking size.

Nutrition: Calories 38; Fat 3.3g; Fiber 0.4g; Carbs 1g; Protein 1.4g;

Ultimate Skillet Brownies

Prep T: 15 min | Cook T: 40 min | Servings: 6

Ingredients

- 64 g all-purpose flour
- 32 g unsweetened cocoa powder
- 3⁄4 tsp sea salt
- 2 large eggs
- 1 tbsp water
- 64 g granulated sugar
- 64 g dark brown sugar
- 1 tbsp vanilla extract
- 227 g semisweet chocolate chips, melted
- 96 g unsalted butter, melted
- Nonstick cooking spray

Directions

1. Whisk the cocoa powder, flour and salt in a bowl.
2. In a large bowl, whisk eggs, water, sugar, brown sugar, and vanilla until smooth.
3. In a microwave-safe bowl, melt now the chocolate in the microwave. In a microwave-safe separate bowl, melt the butter.
4. In a separate bowl, stir the chocolate and butter until evenly combined. Whisk into the egg mixture. Now add the dry ingredients slowly, stirring just until incorporated.
5. Place the baking pan on the bake position. Select Bake, set the temperature to 350 F (177 C), and set the time to 40 min.
6. Lightly grease the baking pan with cooking spray. Pour the batter into the pan, spreading evenly.
7. Bake for 40 min.
8. After 40 min, check that baking is complete. A wooden toothpick inserted in the center of the brownies should come out clean.

Nutrition: Calories 383; Fat 28 g; Carbohydrates 27 g; Protein 5 g; Fiber 1.3 g; Sugar 12 g;

White milk donut

Prep T: 20 min | Cook T: 35 min | Servings: 4

Ingredients

- 200 g of egg whites
- 60 g of sugar
- 120 ml of milk
- 200 g of flour
- 10 g of baking powder
- 3 tbsp granulated sugar
- An 20 cm donut mold

Directions

1. In a planetary mixer or with the aid of an electric whisk, whip egg whites and sugar, then at low speed, add the flour and the sifted yeast a little at a time. When the mixture is smooth, add the milk while whipping at a low speed. Pour into the greased and floured mold.
2. On the surface, sprinkle with sugar grains.
3. In the air fryer at 150 C/300 F, cook for approx. 35 min. If you want a more decisive browning, increase the temperature a little in the last few min.

Nutrition: Calories 181; Fat 13 g; Carbohydrates 1 g; Sugar 4 g; Protein 3 g;

Middle East Baklava

Prep T: 10 min | Cook T: 16 min | Servings: 10

Ingredients

- 128 g walnut pieces
- 128 g shelled raw pistachios
- 64 g unsalted butter, melted
- 32 g plus 2 tps of honey, divided
- 3 tbsp granulated sugar
- 1 tsp ground cinnamon
- 2 (54-g) packages frozen miniature phyllo tart shells

Directions

1. Place the walnuts and pistachios in the air fry basket in an even layer.
2. Place the basket on the air fry position.
3. Select Air Fry, set the temperature to 350 F (180 C), and set the time for 4 min.
4. After 2 min, remove the basket and stir the nuts. Transfer now the basket back to the air fryer grill and cook for another 1 to 2 min until the nuts are golden brown color and fragrant.
5. Meanwhile, stir together the butter, sugar, cinnamon, and 32 g of honey in a medium bowl.
6. When done, remove the basket from the air fryer grill and place the nuts on a cutting board and allow to cool for 5min. Finely chop the nuts. Add the chopped nuts and all the "nut dust" to the butter mixture and stir well.
7. Arrange the phyllo cups on the basket. Evenly fill the phyllo cups with the nut mixture, mounding it up. As you work, stir the nuts in the bowl frequently so that the syrup is evenly distributed throughout the filling.
8. Place the basket on the bake position.
9. Select Bake, set temperature to 350 F (180 C), and set time to 12 min. After about 8 min, check the cups. Continue cooking until the cups are golden brown and the syrup is bubbling.
10. When cooking is complete, remove the baklava from the air fryer grill, drizzle each cup with about 1/8 tsp of the remaining honey over the top.
11. Allow to cool down for 5 min before serving.

Nutrition: Calories 136.6; Fat 11.4 g; Carbohydrates 8.2 g; Protein 0.4 g; Fiber 0.1 g; Sugar 4.4 g;

Cranberry Chocolate Cupcakes

Prep T: 5 min | Cook T: 20 min |Serving: 6

Ingredients

Cupcakes:
- 96 g self-rising flour
- 96 g caster sugar
- 32 g cocoa powder
- A pinch of sea salt
- A pinch of grated nutmeg
- 2 eggs, whisked
- 64 g buttermilk
- 1/2 stick butter, melted
- 56 g dried cranberries

Frosting:
- 64 g butter, room temperature
- 1tsp vanilla extract
- 85 g chocolate chips, melted
- 4tbsp heavy whipping cream

Directions

1. Start now by preheating your Air Fryer to 165 C/330 F.
2. Mix all the ingredients for the cupcakes. Scrape the batter into silicone baking molds; place them in the Air Fryer basket.
3. Bake your cupcakes for about 15 min or until a tester comes out dry and clean.
4. Beat all the ingredients for the frosting using an electric mixer. Pipe the frosting onto the cupcakes.

Nutrition: Calories: 545; Fat; 54.4g; Carbs; 6.2g; Protein; 36g; Sugars; 3.1g; Fiber: 13g;

Simple Chocolate Cupcakes with Blueberries

Prep T: 5 min | Cook T: 15 min | Servings: 6

Ingredients

- 96 g granulated erythritol
- 160 g almond flour
- 1 tsp unsweetened baking powder
- 3 tsps cocoa powder
- 1/2 tsp baking soda
- 1/2 tsp ground cinnamon
- 1/4 tsp grated nutmeg
- 1/8 tsp salt
- 64 ml milk
- 1 stick butter, at room temperature
- 3 eggs, whisked
- 1 tsp pure rum extract
- 64 g blueberries
- Cooking Spray

Directions

1. Spray a 6-cup muffin tin with some cooking spray.
2. In a mixing bowl, combine the erythritol, almond flour, cocoa powder, baking powder, baking soda, nutmeg, cinnamon, and salt and stir until well blended.
3. In another mixing bowl, mix together the eggs, butter, milk, and rum extract until thoroughly combined. Slowly and carefully pour this mixture in the bowl of dry mixture. Stir in the blueberries.
4. Spoon the batter in the greased muffin cups, filling each about three-quarters full.
5. Place the muffin tin on the bake position.
6. Select Bake, set temperature to 345 F (174 C), and set time to 15 min.
7. When done, the center should be springy and a toothpick inserted in the middle should come out clean.
8. Remove from the air fryer grill and place on a wire rack to cool. Serve immediately.

Conversion Table

Volume Equivalents (Liquid)

US STANDARD

US STANDARD (OUNCES)

METRIC (APPROXIMATE)

2 tbsp

1 fl. oz.
30 mL

1/4 cup

2 fl. oz.
60 mL

1/2 cup

4 fl. oz.
120 mL

1 cup

8 fl. oz.
240 mL

11/2 cups

12 fl. oz.
355 mL

2 cups or 1 pint

16 fl. oz.
475 mL

4 cups or 1 quart

32 fl. oz.
1 L

1 gallon

128 fl. oz.
4 L

Volume Equivalents (Dry)

US STANDARD

METRIC (APPROXIMATE)

1/8 tsp

0.5 mL

1/4 tsp

1 mL

1/2 tsp

2 mL

3/4 tsp

4 mL

1 tsp

5 mL

1 tbsp

15 mL

1/4 cup

59 mL

1/3 cup

79 mL

1/2 cup

118 mL

2/3 cup

156 mL

3/4 cup

177 mL

1 cup

235 mL

2 cups or 1 pint

475 mL

3 cups

700 mL

4 cups or 1 quart

1 L

Oven Temperatures

FAHRENHEIT (F)

CELSIUS (C) (APPROXIMATE)

250°F

120°C

300°F

150°C

325°F

165°C

350°F

180°C

375°F

190°C

400°F

200°C

425°F

220°C

450°F

230°C

Index

Golden Vegetarian Meatballs	35
Greek Eggplant Rounds	32
Green Beans Salad	23
Green Curry Shrimp	65

H

Halibut Steaks	59
Ham and Cheese Stuffed Chicken	37
Hearty Turkey Burger	39
Honey-Glazed Roasted Vegetables	34

L

Lamb Stew	54
Lamb and Feta Hamburgers	47
Lemon and Butter Artichok	29
Lemon-Blueberry Muffins	13
Lemon-Pepper Chicken Wings	38
Lemony Raspberry Muffins	67
Lime and Mozzarella Eggplants	23

M

Mexican Topped Avocados	34
Middle East Baklava	74
Mixed Veggies	29
Mozzarella Almond Bagels	19
Mozzarella Meatball Sandwiches with Basil	53
Mushroom Cakes	28

N

Nutty Granola	16

O

Oaty Chocolate Cookies	71
Orange Cinnamon Cookies	72

P

Pancake Cake	13
Panko-Crusted Beef Steaks	49
Panko-Crusted Lamb Rack	52
Paprika Shrimp	64
Parmesan Crusted Pork Chops	48
Parmesan Salmon Fillets	58
Pork Loin Roast with Spice Rub	54
Pork Taquitos	55
Pork Tenders with Bell Peppers	55
Pound Cake with Mixed Berries	70

R

Ranch Tilapia	59
Raspberry Pop-Tarts	70
Rosemary Balsamic Glazed Beet	33

Rosemary Garlic Potatoes	24

S

Salmon Burgers	62
Salmon and Creamy Chives Sauce	61
Sausage and Cheese Balls	15
Sesame Chicken Thighs	44
Simple Balsamic-Glazed Carrots	26
Simple Chocolate Cupcakes with Blueberries	75
Smoked Asparagus	23
Spiced Pudding	21
Spicy Kale Chips	35
Spinach Zucchini Casserole	19
Sponge Cake	69
Strawberry Cups	70
Sumptuous Seafood Casserole	63
Sweet and Spicy Turkey Meatballs	40
Swiss chard and Sausage	17

T

Tender Spicy Chicken	38
Teriyaki Salmon with Bok Choy	59
Tilapia Tacos	61
Tofu Scramble	17
Tuna Steaks with Red Onions	62

U

Ultimate Skillet Brownies	73

W

Walnut Pancake	14
White Wine Chicken Breast	41
White milk donut	73

Z

Zucchini and Potato Tots	27

Printed in Great Britain
by Amazon

83393086R00045